COLLINS GUIDE
TO WILD HABITATS

D1497087

SHORELANDS–
ROCKY

RIGHT **Hermit Crab**

COLLINS GUIDE
TO WILD HABITATS

CHRIS
PACKHAM

With 70 colour photographs
by the author and 4 colour
plates by Chris Shields

LEFT **Cliffscape**
RIGHT **Mermaid's Tresses**

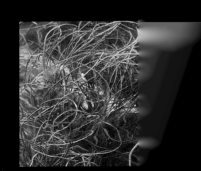

COLLINS
Grafton Street

This book is for my friend and
fellow naturalist Sir Newton
Rycroft, Bart., whose cumulative
knowledge and madcap
enthusiasm have been of great
inspiration since our first literary
tirades.

William Collins Sons & Co Ltd
London · Glasgow · Sydney · Auckland
Toronto · Johannesburg
Text and photographs © 1989 Chris Packham
Colour plates © 1989 Chris Shields

First edition 1989

Art Editor: Caroline Hill
Designer: Judith Robertson

ISBN 0 00 219842 8 Paperback
ISBN 0 00 219868 1 Hardback
Filmset by Ace Filmsetting Ltd, Frome,
Somerset
Colour origination by
Wace Litho, Birmingham, UK
Printed and bound by
New Interlitho SpA, Milan, Italy

CONTENTS

RIGHT **Snakelock's Anemone**

Acknowledgements are due, as ever to John Buckley for his effervescent ecological enthusiasm; to Andrew Welch for continued parasitic access to his library; to Barbara Levy for stomaching my other literary inventions; to Graham Roberts of Fareham Cameras, for years of photographic support; to Jane Harvey of Canon (UK) Ltd, for loan of photographic equipment; to Julian Cremona for reading sections of salty sodden balderdash; to the Sealife Centres at Portsmouth and Weymouth; especially to Stephen 'Scalectrix' Bolwell, a man who knows a piece of rust when he sees it; to my parents for greeting my toys with the same enthusiasm as they poured on my ladybirds, grass snakes and record collection!; to the Prettiest star, shimmering somewhere; to the Tiny Twinkleheart; and to Jenny for playing Sealand when I needed it most.

ACKNOWLEDGEMENTS

LEFT **Lesser Black-backed Gull**

GENESIS

The forces of creation. A grinding of the elements. Land, sea and sky rage in anarchic fusion. Anger, violence, simplicity and power. The atmosphere becomes ocean through driving hail. Solid crystals of sky ricochet off the basalt precipices and dissolve in the furious salty surf. Liquid crashes against solid and their molecules mix in a million tons of deafening abrasion. This is pure physics in collision at the height of a storm. Dangerous explosions of incomprehensible force erupt on all sides as you stand in the painful blurring of reality, on top of a cliff staring into the wrath of the Atlantic. Offshore in the dirge of grey and green there is a momentary lull and a fork of lightning pulses from the illuminated sea, freezing for a second massive, dusty-jade waves and fragments of foam. It could have been lightning that was life giving, which linked molecules in a primeval soup at the instant of creation.

But around you there is not a single sign of life, past or present. No plants, birds, or animals, no carcasses of failed forms. Nothing it appears can survive this severity. This hostile promontory is where the adaptive arrogance of Mother Earth has met its match and lost. A last bastion of total inorganic purity, or so it appears, because when the tumult subsides to calm, the shore will be littered with the casualties of one of the richest of all our environments. Communities of plants and animals which are currently being chastised by the tempest will magically appear, the sky will ring with pealing cries from thousands of birds and the man who would be God will stand small, 3,500 million years too late, amidst the most ancient of terrestrial habitats, the coast.

Coastland can be flats of shimmering sand, miles of rancid mud or banks and spits of rumbling shingle, but by far the most spectacular are the steep terraces of broken land, some with sheer drops of

LEFT **A party of Eiders**
RIGHT **Gannet aggression**

1. ON THE WATERFRONT

over a hundred metres, those stark and brutal bulwarks we call cliffs. To stand on top of these in the throes of a winter gale is about as close to nature as you can get, so close in fact that you are faced with the basics of geology before botany or zoology can breathe in your mind. Coastal cliffs are invaluable to the geologist for revealing the secrets of the earth's crust, but in the storm it is erosion which predominates.

SOME GEOLOGY

Despite the buffetting clouds of spray and huge size of some of the breaking waves, the actual eroding force of the sea is targeted at a very small area at the foot of the cliff. As each wave pounds inshore a mass of water and trapped air is flung at the rock face and tremendous forces are exacted on any tiny crack, cranny or fissure. The back of the cliff is gradually broken and undermined into a narrow notch which runs around its base. From above this, loosened rocks collapse to be ground into sand and, albeit slowly, the land shrinks backwards under the might of the sea. Any joints, faults, or lines of weaker rock are eroded more quickly and often expanded into caves, and when these are tunnelled inland and the land here collapses, a blowhole is produced. From here, during a storm, clouds of water pulse up in a billowing, salty geyser yet one such blow-hole I have seen has a busy colony of drenched Kittiwakes nesting in it. They spin, screaming, deep down into this tube of sandstone to disappear into a flickering rainbow of spray.

When two opposing caves run parallel with the cliff great arches are sometimes formed, and when the roofs of these eventually collapse stacks are left as great columns rising from the sea. The Old Man of Hoy on Orkney is at least 140 metres high, sticking up like a broken finger of red sandstone gesturing defiantly at the elements. His fate is sealed, however, because eventually his hard base will be beaten and scoured away and he will

crumble into the sea as a New Man of Hoy begins to evolve elsewhere. Many of these seaside sculptures have famous names. Durdle Dor in Dorset is an arch and stack structure formed of Portland stone; the Mupe Rocks further along the coast are a neat row of stacks lacing 500 metres of the English Channel; Den's Door in Pembrokeshire is another famous stack; and further along this coast is the huge Green Bridge of Wales, a giant arch leaping out of the crumbling cliff. These natural tower blocks and fly-overs are often squatted upon by nesting seabirds who enjoy the less severe summer weather and essential protection from four-legged predators. Cliffs can be formed where softer rocks, clays or sand line the sea, typically on the east coast, but here landslips are far more frequent and the dramatic scenery that typifies the cliffland of Britain's western coasts never evolves from the erosion.

The oldest rocks which are mixed into the modern British Isles are about three thousand million years old, but it was only sixty million years ago that Britain rose from the sea in its present form. Indeed during the last six hundred million years Britain has drifted all the way from the South Pole up through the equator, where it enjoyed a little two hundred million year holiday, to its current latitude. It has endured a range of hot and cold seas and climates, been burned by volcanoes, bashed by plate movements, had mountains made and then flattened into seas, lakes and deserts, and finally has been periodically iced over. Our isles have been part of Canada and Greenland, had a fling with Scandinavia, frequently fell out with Scotland which was initially another continent, and have been continually in and out of water. We now roam over the vestiges of the Caledonian mountains, St George's land, the Variscan Mountains, the London Platform, the Wealdon deltas and the deposits of the Pleistocene glacials. Since the end of the last Ice Age ten thousand years ago we have entered the recent or Holocene time period. Considering what has gone before, we now so arrogantly presume that the world has stopped for us. Yet the movements which forced our countries from one side of the globe to another are still in action and the forces of evolution which shape all of the organisms which now cover the land are equally dynamic. We are not the final product of this little earth, and nor are any of the animals and plants which currently live here. We are just fortunate enough to be looking at life in a tiny slice of time, life which will continue to change and re-evolve long after the British Isles have sunk beneath the sea, been buried by another Ice Age or forced by plate movements back into the southern seas.

Having said this, the coast is the best place to admire the enormous range of life which currently climbs, clambers, creeps or crawls on our planet. It is always edges of ecotypes which are the richest; where woodland mixes with meadow, where scrub mixes with grassland, or where wet heath mixes with dry. It is at such places that there are not only the two groups of species from either side of the ecocline but a host of others which exploit the best of both worlds. At the seaside, where not only two ecotypes, but two states of matter are adjacent, we naturally find the richest variety of all of our planet's multitudes of lifeforms. On the shore you can discover members from groups and classes of animals and plants which are almost entirely confined to the depths of the seas. Amongst the rocks they struggle under the hostile conditions of the rising and falling tides. Yet sea urchins, starfish, brittlestars, sea cucumbers, corals, sea anemones and jellyfish can all be seen in this arena filled by two great environments. Joining these are those species which have evolved to exploit both the land and the sea. Otters transform from land-loving lopers into flex-

Out to the sea

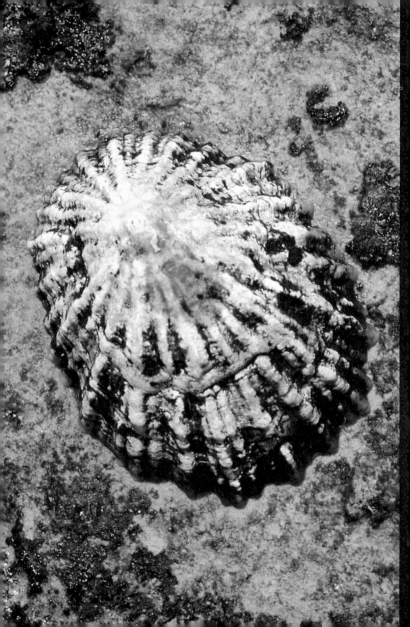

ing metal eels underwater; seals, those sleek, slippery and streamlined mammals, wriggle ashore to breed. Meanwhile the skies are filled with the massive numbers of seabirds who return to breed in summer. But these are the vertebrate exotics. There are a whole range of organisms which many of us sneer at and tread over in the pursuit of our own particular gems of nature. The next time you creep across the shore to glimpse a gull, or a seal pup, or scan about for an otter, spare a thought for the limpet. The limpet, that stoic, crusty cone which remains stuck to the rocks in the most hideous storms and is really not such a monotonous mollusc.

THE LIMPET

The most frequently encountered species is the Common Rock Limpet *Patella vulgata*, which has a nearly round conical shell, varying in colour from olive to chocolate dashed with rays of grey, white and brown on the many ribs which radiate from the apex of the cone and give the shell its strength. Common Rock Limpets can be found glued to rocks on all but the most exposed or sheltered beaches, and their shells can sometimes grow to measure 7 centimetres across. Beneath this the actual animal, which most of us go a lifetime without seeing, is a dusky blue colour and has two long, eyed tentacles which fold neatly away under the shell. Its lips are thick and puckered, its jaws dark grey, and its extraordinarily long tongue a brownish-amber. This ribbon-like appendage has 160 rows of hooked teeth, 12 to a row and is known as a radula. Using the radula the limpet rasps and scours away at the surface of the rock, licking up any algae or detritus growing there. The animal edges forward on its powerful muscular 'foot', leaving its tongue hanging out behind it. It then draws this back into its mouth leaving a tell-tale trail which traces its wanderings.

LEFT **A limpet – not such a monotonous mollusc**

When limpets live on calcareous rocks such as chalk, they often excavate a depression for themselves to sit snuggly into. After feeding they will return to this pock mark in the rock to idle away the dry hours of their life, when the tide is out. The depression is produced using a combination of weak carbonic acid (produced when they respire) and the grinding action of the shell on the rock while it is being pounded by the force of the waves. During such onslaughts limpets use the strength of their feet to anchor themselves to the rock. At low tide the ability to hug the rock very closely helps them withstand seabird attacks, changes in temperature, the effects of desiccation and also protects them from any poisonous fresh water which could seep under their shells. However, they do not always clamp on tightly because limpets can breathe in air, as well as respire using gills under water.

Sexes are separate and reproduction normally takes place in spring. The eggs and sperms are released into the sea and, after fertilization, these develop into millions of microscopic larvae which form part of the drifting plankton fauna. Huge losses are suffered before these settle on the shoreline and develop into juvenile limpets, but this apparently wasteful method of reproduction is used so that the young limpets have a separate habitat, and source of food, from the adults and competition is thus reduced.

Although they are too leathery to be anyone's delicacy today, in the past limpets were collected in Ireland for food and in other parts of Britain for fishing bait. In the 1850s twelve million limpets a year were collected around Berwick and the population took a dramatic plunge. But those were the days of some pretty serious shore searching and from Dover to Oban parties of naturalists were enthusing about the weird and wonderful inhabitants of our rocky shores. For any modern badger- or birdwatcher, botanist or bluebottle fancier a first peer into a rock-pool can be like a view of another world.

A giant, glassy form wobbles through green to brown. It is a visitor from another world, held on many limbed extensions of amber crystal, each studded at its joint by a pinhead of gold, each a tiny slither of translucence. Gently the monster perambulates over the smooth surface of the rock, at times it almost disappears, at times so obvious, like a living lens which scintillates the few sunspots which puncture the dingy and waxy weeds. Suddenly, in its skin, a cohesive fusion of thousands of swelling tiny black spots causes the creature to lose its shine. It becomes as sullen as the weed which brushes its sides, and then it disappears. Ghosts of this visitor scatter the floor, lifeless, milky reminders which sway in unison with the waves, tumbling over and across the sand.

As the monster vanishes a crimson-spotted cushion everts a hundred bending soft spines, pneumatic tubes of green. Tinged with purple, tipped with poison, they tower high over a carpet of tiny green volcanoes. From around the edge of a canyon a sandstone robot in a barbed helmet sidles into view. Armed with pincing weapons it is scarred with living white stones, which flick fans like radar antennae on paranoid tanks.

Finally after a slippery struggle through a grove of olive-green bubbled leaves and a careering dive into near darkness the most hideous form is confronted. A giant globe of glowing spines. Pastel pink and mauve, with an aura of elastic fibres tipped with tiny torches, all enveloping a dense core of pulsing red.

This tangle of images, halfway between a nightmare and a dream, are not visions of a distant planet, or a futuristic invasion of our own by aliens, but only a view into an average rock-pool. A change of dimension from air to water and a change of scale can transform a Common Prawn *Palaemon serratus* into a weird glassy giant wandering amongst his fellows' shed skins.

LEFT **The feathery Plumose Anemone**

15

Dahlia Anemone

Snakelocks Anemones *Anemonia sulcata*, Edible Crabs *Cancer pagurus* and their barnacle guests *Balanus* spp., Breadcrumb Sponges *Halichondria panicea* and an Edible Sea Urchin *Echinus esculentus* become outrageous entities without the use of give-away key words such as tentacles, pincers, shells and testes. Yet today, in the ecology conscious eighties, these species and a myriad of their cohabitants are largely ignored by the general naturalist. A hundred years ago the coast was alive with the billowing petticoats of Victorian ladies, each clutching baskets laden with shore life, leaping from rock to rock in frustrated pursuit of their menfolk. The wonders of the sea shore were the opium of the age and inspired by the writings of one Phillip Henry Gosse, the Victorians first enthused and then abused, in their customary manner of over-collecting, this delicate landscape. Indeed Gosse's son, Edmund, was ridden with guilt when he wrote 'No one will see again on the shore of England what I saw in my early childhood, the submarine vision of

dark rocks, speckled and starred with an infinite variety of colour, and streamed by silken flags of royal crimson and purple'. Luckily a vestige of these halcyon days still remains, and there is plenty for us to explore today. A useful tip here is to go equipped with a scuba-diving face-mask. Even though you do not intend to submerge yourself fully, this will help you see through the ripples on the water and reduce any confusing reflections.

The same forces of erosion which have shaped the beach also create the rockpools, which can vary from a small depression or angular crevice in a single slab of rock, to large expanses of water which may be several metres deep. Pools encountered at the top of the shore usually suffer extreme variations in conditions, and thus usually have only filmy types of blue-green and green seaweeds, such as *Enteromorpha*, and their animal fauna is composed mainly of small crustaceans such as Sea Slaters *Ligia oceanica*, Springtails *Anurida maritima* and the occasional Shore Crab *Carcinus maenas*.

Beadlet Anemone

Further down the beach where pools are regularly covered and in turn exposed to the elements there is a far greater diversity of life. Although they appear to be full of *Lithophyllum* seaweed, which forms a pinkish encrustation over the rocks, these pools in fact hold the most diverse displays of rock-pool life. But existence here is not easy. The shore is, after all, the strip where the argumentative elements abut to create a hostile cline between sea and land. Rock-pools in fact endure an even harsher environment than the open sea because they are faced with a series of oscillations which rack their stability. Their temperature, salinity, acidity and gaseous conditions continually vary, mainly due to their sealed nature, and their smaller scale which precludes any of the dilutive effects available to the oceans.

Temperature can vary dramatically in pools at the upper reaches of the beach, because here the water is quickly warmed by the summer sun at low tide, and then violently cooled when the sea returns. In winter, when the air is generally cooler than the sea, the reverse occurs, and the incoming tide brings warmth. During the summer, heating of these pools causes evaporation and the salinity rises because they may spend long periods of time without the refreshing influence of the sea. The acidity and gaseous conditions of the pool also vary, due to the dense populations of animals and plants which occur in these restricted volumes of water. During the day the plants use the energy from the sunlight to photosynthesise, just as terrestrial plants do, and liberate oxygen into the water, whilst reducing the concentration of carbon dioxide. The animals present respire just as we do and thus use up this oxygen, whilst producing carbon dioxide, water and other waste materials. Thus during daylight the amount of acidic carbon dioxide in the water is reduced, whilst oxygen accumulates: at night the reverse occurs and carbon dioxide levels increase. Thus the pool varies from alkaline during the day to increasingly acid at night.

Such dramatic fluctuations have a dominant effect on the ecology of the pools

because many organisms are not adapted to live under such a variable set of conditions, even though the changes are cyclical, such as day–night or tide-related events. As ever, though evolution triumphs over adversity and a myriad of species flourish in a semi-submarine existence.

SOME ROCK-POOL BEAUTIES

The generally dull and grimy-coloured seaweeds, to be considered later, have no need of colourful flowers because their pollination is active and unaided by any animal vectors. Thus the brighter spectacles of the pools are provided by animals like the beautiful, yellow Sea Lemon *Archidoris pseudoargus*, a sea slug, whose coarse back is spotted with patches of green, mauve or crimson. These hermaphrodites sport fine, feathery gills which frill around their backs as they creep over sponges and weeds before, after a single year, they spawn and die. Longer lived and lovelier still are the sea anemones. Their startling yet subtly tinged tentacles almost seem to luminesce as they flounce about in the dusky currents of the pool.

These anemones are hollow cylindrical animals which firmly attach to the rock or seaweed using their strong and muscular pedal disc bases. At the opposite end a ring of tentacles surrounds a mouth, which opens into a central gastric cavity. This stomach is partitioned by a series of ribbon-like filaments which increase the surface area for digestion of the animal's food. Between this and the tough rubbery outer layer is a jelly-like filling called the mesogloea, and this unusually elastic substance stiffens the anemone without preventing changes of size and shape. Sea anemones also have muscles and nerve cells which enable them to move parts of their bodies in a co-ordinated way. They normally reproduce sexually. Eggs and sperm are released into the gastric cavity and are then ejected through the mouth of

LEFT **Beadlet Anemone**

the anemone into the open sea. Here in the abyss of the ocean fertilisation occurs and a tiny ciliated larva grows before later settling on the rock and developing into an adult anemone.

The anemone's prettiness is deceptive, because in the rock-pool habitat they are very effective carnivores. Some eat quite large crustaceans, such as shrimps, and small fishes whilst others only prey upon minute members of the zooplankton. All have a unique and unhealthy (for the prey) method of predation. When a potential meal touches the unfolded tentacles, thousands of tiny cells discharge stinging harpoons which attach the prey to the tentacles and inject it with venom. These devilish little weapons are called nematocysts and are small fluid-filled structures, inside which is a long coiled filament. Many thousands of these coat each tentacle and each is equipped with its own trigger hair. When prey passes by, this hair detects it either by touch or smell, and triggers the cell into a chemical reaction. The permeability of the tiny capsule wall increases and water rushes in. The change is so rapid that the nematocysts discharge incredibly quickly, the filaments shooting out, piercing the skin of the victim and attaching to the flesh by means of small, backward pointing barbs. Simultaneously they inject a paralysing or lethal venom which destroys the nervous system, stimulates the shedding of limbs and produces violent convulsions. From the prawn's point of view this is a very unfriendly mixture of toxins.

Many species of anemone can be found around our shores but the Beadlet Anemone *Actinia equina* is the most common and familiar. It has a variable colouring, but is easily identified by a ring of blue worts lying at the base of each tentacle. Although this species can be found in quite large aggregations above or below the water-line they are also somewhat territorial. If another anemone attaches too close to its neighbour a fight may develop. Each anemone will sting the other for two or three minutes before the loser detaches from the substrate and drifts away. Of the two colour forms that occur, red and green, the green anemones seem far more placid and rarely fight amongst themselves.

Another conspicuous species is the Snakelocks Anemone *Anemonia sulcata* which cannot survive for long out of water because its long tentacles cannot be fully retracted. This species lives in crannies and cracks at the bottom of pools, but unlike most anemones it also attaches in the brightest lit areas and spreads its tentacles towards the light. The arms have vast numbers of brown algae living inside them in a partnership of mutual aid, or symbiosis. The algal cells gain protection and are also able to tap a rich source of carbon dioxide and nutrients, produced by the sea anemone as waste, which they need for the formation of organic compounds. The anemone on the other hand profits by an automatic removal of the waste products of its chemical activities and possibly is supplied with some of its nutrients by the brown algae's metabolism.

Common Prawn

PRAWNS AND CRABS

The next time you delicately peel a prawn in a restaurant spare a thought for the poor beast's discarded limbs. Indeed take the trouble to defy etiquette and dissect your *hors-d'œuvres* on the side of the plate; I have no doubt you will be amazed by the complicated morphology of the twenty pairs of appendages which occur along the segments of its, albeit tasty, body. Starting from the front, the first pair are the antennules, which are used as organs of balance, these are followed by the antennae, which are sensory organs and then six pairs of modified limbs arranged around the mouth. These include the biting jaws or mandibles, the maxillipeds, which are used to hold and manipulate the food and, between these, the maxillae, which pump water over the gills. Next come four pairs of walking legs, followed by five pairs of swimming limbs and terminally a complicated tail. All of this discarded tissue will make a confusing pile on the side of your plate, has provided countless A-level Zoology students with nightmares, and has been pulled from a highly specialised animal which deserves more attention than just being a gastronomic delicacy.

Prawns spend the winter in the warmth and protection of the open ocean, but during early spring they migrate to cooler, coastal pools often seeking those high up on the shore. Here they can be difficult to see because of their transparency and habit of hiding in weeds, but once discovered are worthy of examination. Of all their limbs only the three hind-most pairs of the walking legs are employed for walking whilst the first pair are armed with fine nippers which serve to pick up pieces of weed or animal debris which are passed to the feeding appendages near the mouth. Like all of their kind, prawns are scavengers, detecting their food using conspicuous eyes, mounted on moveable stalks, and by the enlarged and elaborate antennae, which have three branches enabling the animal to scour every bit of its environment. When disturbed their broad tail-fan is opened out, and the whole abdomen bends suddenly under the body, causing the creature to shoot violently backwards, with all its appendages trailing out behind the moving body. Now their five pairs of swimming limbs are used, each interlocked by little spines which give them the appearance of holding hands. These beat rhythmically and the prawn moves gently through the water until it lands again. These paddles are then turned back flat against the undersurface of the tail to allow it to walk on its legs.

All crustaceans have a jointed exterior skeleton which is like an inflexible suit of armour. In order to grow they need to shed this constricting skin and during the summer this process occurs about every two weeks. When the prawn is ready to moult, a dark or obscure cranny is sought out and in just twenty seconds the shell of the prawn splits across the back and a soft, yet perfect, reproduction of the original animal slips out in a sudden upward jerk. The cuticle of the microscopic eyes, of the hairs and appendages on the body, and even of the stomach, which is armed with teeth and elaborate filters, is shed in this incredible process. Immediately the animal swells and the new soft shell stretches over the surface of the enlarging body. After only a short pause the animal can

swim. A few hours later the mouthparts have hardened enough for it to feed. Two days later the shell or carapace is as hard as its predecessor, which now lies as litter on the bottom of the rock-pool. In females this amazing process is further enhanced by a special moult which gives rise to a series of long hairs which are attached to the rear part of the abdomen. After such a moult the soft female is immediately mated by a male who plasters his sperm near the entrance to her ovaries. Egg laying begins straight away and the female stands motionless fanning a steady stream of eggs back across the fertilising sperm and into the swimming appendages. Here the eggs accumulate in a dark mass and are cemented to the hairs by a glue prepared in the swimming legs. As many as three thousand are so attached and this whole process is completed in just one hour. Eventually young prawns hatch out as microscopic swimming larva, swelling the numbers of the temporary plankton in the pool. A short while after this the female moults again losing her breeding fringes. In the autumn she, and all the other females which have survived the summer

Edible Crab

in the rock-pools, move out to the open sea for another restorative winter.

Closely related to prawns are the crabs, those arrogant and aggressive marauders of seaside detritus. If prawns are manic and lobsters foul-tempered, then crabs are cheeky, always lurking or dancing about waving their petulant pincers at almost any assailant. Although they can be found under rocks at the top of the shore most species are confined to the deep rock-pools near the level of the lowest tide, where they are often effectively camouflaged by thick growths of weed, sponges or barnacles which attach themselves to the shell, or carapace, of the crab. Shore Crabs *Carcinus maenas* are the most familiar and hardy of the British species, but Edible Crabs *Cancer pagurus* may also be found in the summer near the low tide mark. Porcelain crabs *Porcellana* spp. are very well adapted to life on the shore, because they have a flattened body and claws and sharply pointed legs which enable them to cling tightly to boulders and avoid being swept away by waves. Like some lizard species, such as the Common Lizard *Lacerta vivipara*, many crabs have a defence mechanism which involves shedding part of or even an entire limb. When threatened by seabirds or fish this is snapped off by a sudden muscle contraction at a specific breaking point near the base of the limb segment and this process, known as autotomy, is designed to save the life of the crab by distracting the predator's attention to the more minor meal. The resulting wound is immediately sealed and later during the moult a new limb is grown, although it takes several moults before it attains its full size.

BARNACLES

These are another crustacean which can be found in tens of thousands on the rocky shore. They are often presumed to be molluscs and related to such animals as the limpets, Archaeogastropoda, but their stationary, shelled existence has evolved as a protection against predators, wave action, and desiccation after the retreat of the tides. In some places these animals coat the rocks like a coarse granular icing, which is sharp to touch and will skin your knees should you stumble. They will also grow on some seaweeds and the slower moving crustaceans. Those found on rocky shores are unstalked and known as acorn barnacles. These are composed of a circle of shell plates, usually six, which are attached to the rock at the barnacle's head. Four more plates form a trap door at the top of this pyramidal structure, and this opens when the tide is in, allowing the highly modified legs to be pushed out so the barnacle can feed. There are six pairs of limbs, three short and three long, and all are fringed by structures called setae. Once the trap door opens the three pairs of long limbs unroll, and are repeatedly thrust forward with their setae extended so that any particles in their path are apt to be caught, passed to the mouth and swallowed. Such a frenetic fanning movement causes a current of water over the barnacle which ensures that water is never refiltered, and in just one hour a single barnacle can thoroughly filter 10 cubic centimetres of sea water. From this they extract protozoa and small crustaceans such as the larvae of crabs and prawns.

The Common Acorn Barnacle *Balanus balanoides* can be found on the midshore all around our coast, whilst the Star Barnacle *Chthamalus stellatus* is found on the more exposed, western shores. This species is able to survive better at the top of the shore because it can withstand desiccation and extreme temperatures, whilst the former has a porous shell and cannot survive long out of the water. Because the former species has no calcium in its shell it can grow at a faster rate and therefore the Common Acorn outcompetes the Star Barnacle for space by crushing or overgrowing it. Today the Common Acorn Barnacle is facing competition on the midshore zone from an introduced species from Australia, *Elminius modestus*, which has spread from its original site of introduction near Portsmouth, all around the east and west coast of Britain as far as the Shetlands.

FISH

Of the fishes which inhabit our rock-pools many are incredibly well camouflaged. The Shanny *Lipophrys pholis* is extremely common and varies in colour from brown to green depending on its background, often being blotched to break up its body's outline. This species is one of the few that emerge while the pool is being observed, but like many of its rock-pool co-habitants its eyes are on the sides of its head and its vision is extremely acute. Once it has spotted you its movement is similarly acute and the best a noisy and fidgety observer can expect to see of rock-pool fish is a dull flash as they slide into a mat of weed. Possibly the finest mimic of background colour is the Sea Scorpion *Taurulus bubalis* which can vary from a bright, almost luminous green when amongst algae in a shallow pool to a deep olive-brown when under the brown seaweeds, or a brick red when found on the red rocks of the Devon or Pembroke coast. A prickly appearance identifies the species, each of its gills being equipped with a long backward

The Red Gurnard – the walking fish

A cryptic gobie

sweeping spine which, although sharp, is not venomous like those of the seaside stingers the weaver fishes *Trachinus draco* and *Echiichthys vipera*.

The Worm Pipe Fish *Neophis lumbriciformis* is almost impossible to detect when it rests amongst the stems of the brown seaweeds, because its body is not only coloured to match this background but also shaped like the stipes of these plants. When it swims it does so with a slow and graceful swaying motion which resembles that of the seaweeds wafting gently in the rock-pool current.

Other fishes avoid predators by hiding in the crevices of rocks and one, the Butterfish or Gunnel *Pholis gunnellus*, is laterally compressed so it can slip into the smallest of cracks and is also incredibly slippery, being almost impossible to catch by hand and practically mercurial when flapping about in a net. This potholing habit

also helps these fish avoid the destructive force of waves breaking over the pool and sweeping them away, but some other species have solved this problem by evolving highly developed sucker discs on their ventral surfaces with which they can attach themselves firmly and thus safely to the rocky substrate.

The most familiar of this type of fish is the Lumpsucker *Cyclopterus lumpus*, which is also one of the largest fish to be found in British rock-pools, often reaching 50 centimetres in length. Its sucker is formed by a development of the pelvic fin, and once attached the fish requires a considerable force to dislodge it. Lumpsuckers are widespread along our northern coast but less common in the south. They live off-shore for most of the year but in spring they arrive in the shallow, rocky areas of the kelp zone, where they breed. Males in breeding attire have bellies burn-

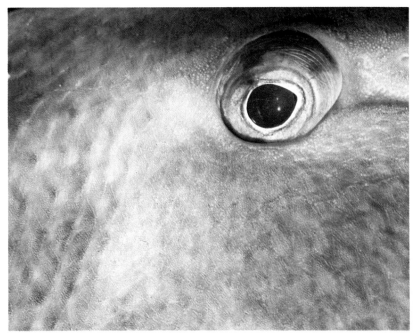

A John Dory

ing with crimson red but this does little to mask the ugliness of this swollen, bulbous-lipped and warty fish. The similarly gross but dour females select the nest-site and deposit several thousand sticky eggs before the male takes charge of the breeding operation by clamping himself to the rock, his head facing the mass of gelatinous cells. These he aerates by fanning his fins and his bright colours and vile appearance probably adequately repulse lesser predators. On hatching the tadpole-like young Lumpsuckers attach themselves to kelp fronds until the end of the summer when they and the adults move into deeper waters. Although these piscine zombies may be occasionally encountered right at the bottom of the beach they are most frequently seen as dead specimens along the strand line. These bloated yet colourful bodies are thought to be casualties of severe weather or the predation of seals.

And so concludes what must be the shallowest of dives into the rock-pool fauna. The splendid urchins; the stomach eversing, predatory array of brittle-stars, sunstars and starfish; the bevy of constructive or destructive worms; the extraordinarily gentle jellyfish; the corals; the chitons; the sea squirts; and of course the massive family of molluscs that graze the forest of seaweeds have all been cast aside at the expense of a skin-shedding shrimp, the stinging cells of an anemone and a few other tiny facets of this alien world. The first time you descend into it you will realise the enormity, the diversity and the marvels this subterranean assembly aspires to. These shallow seaside capsules are full of colour, sharpness, fear, ferocity, tameness and tension. The sky and the sea, the plants and the animals here form a zoological salad with little equal. Go and get wet.

At the foot of the shore, animals and plants are on the brink of two worlds and dependent on the taste of the tide to be tossed into either. You can stand facing the sea as the waves lick your toes with the remarkable rock-pool communities stretching behind you, up the beach. Blue-grey or green, twinkling or sullen the sea appears alien and uninhabited, yet occasionally a few chocolate fronds flicker off-shore. These glimpses are all you will snatch of another environment, they are tips of a forest spending painful seconds out of their natural element. A forest, just like those which cloak the land, here fills a turbulent volume of water. All the competition, evolution and diversity of terrestrial woodland life is duplicated here, where each species has its role as predator, herbivore or decomposer. Flocks of birds are replaced by shoals of fish, swimming through the trees, flying with silver sides through the dense weeds. Weeds, wrapping and wafting in the current, twisting and lifting towards the surface in a struggle for the vestiges of sunlight.

The seaweeds, a whole group of plants which have the common reputation of being brown, smelly and boring. True, some are brown, whilst others are green, blue-green or red. They do smell when rotting on the strand-line, but then so do most things in a state of decay. As for being boring, at a second glance they are far from that. They are the sea's producers, have highly complex sex lives, can withstand ridiculous tidal oppression, are incredibly nutritional and warrant the spending of millions of dollars.

Some of the larger, brown seaweeds, known as kelp (Laminariales), form these dense offshore forests and the most familiar species are Oarweed *Laminaria digitata*, Sugar Kelp *L. saccharina* and Forest Kelp *L. hyperborea*. These species have long wavy fronds with droopy heads

LEFT **The buoyancy aids of the Knotted Wrack**

RIGHT **Red and green seaweed**

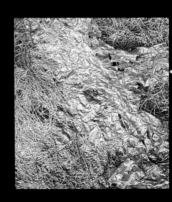

27

and are usually only exposed during the very lowest spring tides. They are attached off-shore to any rocky substrate and thus can be found around most of Britain's coast, with the exception of the south east and East Anglia, which lacks this rocky base. Dependent on photosynthesis, they need sunlight. The plants may grow so close together that they can be impossible to penetrate and, just as in the terrestrial woodland, there are several botanical layers or strata as one rises from the floor to the surface. The rocky surface is often crusted with shade-tolerant seaweeds and these compare with the lichens and mosses in a woodland. Next there is a layer of bushy and foliatious weeds, whose abundance is determined by the amount of available light. A whole host of animal species exists in this colourful layer, which can be compared with the Bluebell, Primrose and Dog's Mercury layer in woodland. The kelp plants themselves form the main body of the canopy, equivalent to terrestrial trees, and these often carry many epiphytic seaweeds which spread their delicate lacework over the fronds. These species benefit not only from their plagiarised food supply, but also by being supported high up in the current of water away from the swirling silt of the bottom. Such a forest is, of course, infested with herbivores, such as sea urchins, limpets, worms, crustaceans and a great range of molluscs. These in turn are preyed upon by birds, fish and other invertebrates, such as starfish: in fact, more than 360 species of animal have been found living in this forest. Finally, and most surprising, just as a tree sheds its leaves, kelp sheds its fronds. During March the enormous masses of seaweed washed up on the beaches are comparable to the swirling autumn leaves of oak, beech and sycamore on the woodland floor.

Seaweeds belong to a family of plants called the Phycophyta, also known as algae. This vast group includes many simple plants without true roots, stems and leaves, many of which are terrestrial or

Bladder Wrack

freshwater single-celled organisms. Seaweeds are generally macroscopic marine algae, which vary in appearance from a simple filament or frond to a crumpled sticky crust which clasps the rock's surface. Their leafy part, the thallus, is a flat sheet of tissue which narrows via the stem or stipe, to a fixing organ known as a holdfast. In the wracks this is no more than a simple disc, but in other species it is a branched root-like attachment, or a layer of tiny sticky filaments growing from a compressed swelling at the base of the stipe. This holdfast uses a powerful glue to secure the seaweed through the extremes of tidal buffeting. In fact seaweeds which grow on really exposed shores can often withstand a pull of 40 kilograms per square centimetre (about 600 pounds per square inch) before their stipe breaks. These plants are further protected by their flexibility and slippery nature which prevents adjacent weeds from rubbing and damaging them when they are swirling together in the tide. This familiar slimeyness also helps the plant to remain elastic, further increasing its resistance to wave action. By exuding slime the plant also rids itself of the hardening compound calcium carbonate which would otherwise accumulate in the plant making it very brittle. The wracks, of which the Channelled Wrack *Pelvetia canaliculata*, Toothed Wrack *Fucus serratus*, and Bladder Wrack *Fucus vesiculosus* are conspicuous around our rocky shores, have a central midrib either side of which are many oval-shaped, air-filled bladders. These bubbles buoy the plant when it is submerged, raising its extremities towards the water surface and the light.

Although seaweeds can be brown, red or even orange, they still contain the all-important, green, photosynthetic compound chlorophyll. In each different seaweed the basic green colour is either masked by several other pigments or, as in red seaweeds, they contain other specialised pigments which absorb every colour except red and violet light. These colours penetrate deeper into the sea than other parts of the spectrum so red weeds are able to grow at depths of up to 350 metres depending on the clarity of the water. Indeed most of the red seaweeds are deep-water plants which grow well below the low water-line, and only a few species can tolerate the high light levels found in rock-pools.

The brown seaweeds are also sensitive to strong sunlight, heat or drying winds, and thus they are normally found on the lower beach, where they sometimes grow in incredibly dense beds of vegetation clothing the surface with an olive-brown slippery blanket. At this density they play a vital part in the ecology of the whole shore. These dense turfs break the force of the waves and surf and in so doing are capable of reducing erosion and stabilising the coast. Whilst protecting the coast itself, these weeds obviously provide pro-

A turf of Toothed Wrack

tection for a wide range of marine life, much of which is very similar to the animals you can find in a rock-pool.

Reproduction in seaweeds can be extremely complicated. In the wracks for instance, male and female organs are on separate plants, situated at the ends of the thallus on small lobed fronds. These bear tiny bulbous fruiting bodies, which are known as recepticals, and each of these has a tiny central opening, or ostiole, which leads to the cavity where the sex organs are formed. Male plants have tiny club-shaped objects called antheridia, whilst females have several pear-shaped sacks known as oogonia, each filled with eggs. When both stages are mature they are washed out into the vastness of the ocean. Such huge numbers are produced that against all odds the tiny male sex cells actually manage to find the eggs and fertilisation is completed. Seaweeds can also reproduce asexually producing spores in special structures called sporangia. When mature these break off from the main body of the plant and form part of the planktonic flora of the sea until they eventually land on a suitable substrate and then grow into mature plants.

Other types of seaweed have an intermediate stage which holds the sexual structures. This too separates from the parent plant and becomes part of the phytoplankton, and only after fertilisation at this stage is a replica of the parent plant able to grow. Developing seaweedlings are very sensitive to water movement, water temperature and salinity, and this has a profound effect on the types of seaweed which can colonise any particular area. Those species most resistant to long periods of exposure to heat and wind are found mostly on the upper shore, whilst those less comfortable with these conditions are found near or below the low water mark. The factors which determine where a particular species of seaweed can grow

are extremely precise. It has been found that Flat or Spiral Wrack *Fucus spiralis* grows well when exposed and immersed for alternating periods of six hours of each. If this time is lengthened to twelve hours the growth rate is reduced to almost nil. The Toothed Wrack *F. serratus*, enjoys its highest growth rate when continually immersed and ceases growing altogether when alternated for a period of six hours. It thus grows under conditions which would kill the Spiral Wrack. This range of variability from the top to the bottom of the shore creates the famous zoning effect of seaweed which can easily be seen from cliff-tops at low tide. Different seaweeds can be identified by their different bands of colour which lace in olive, brown and amber lines along the beach. This phenomenon has provided scientists with an opportunity to categorise and thus this littoral or intertidal environment is divided into four zones.

SHORE ZONATION

At the top of the beach is the splash zone, which is splattered by small amounts of sea water, and can only be populated by species which can withstand extraordinary periods of desiccation. The upper shore zone, often known as the supra-littoral zone, stretches between the average high water mark of the neap tides to the extreme high water mark of the spring tides. There is little marine life here with the exception of the Channelled Wrack which is a hardy, drought-tolerant weed. The middle shore zone, or mid-littoral zone, and the lower shore zone, follow downshore to the surf where the widest range of weeds flourish in minimal exposure. Lastly there is the sub-littoral zone which although never fully exposed may be shallow and it is here that the many tall laminarians occasionally project above the surface at low water.

FOOD AND FARMING

Although seaweed is not a common item in the diet of modern westerners it is gobbled up by the tonne in the east. For the last five

LEFT **Spiral Wrack**

31

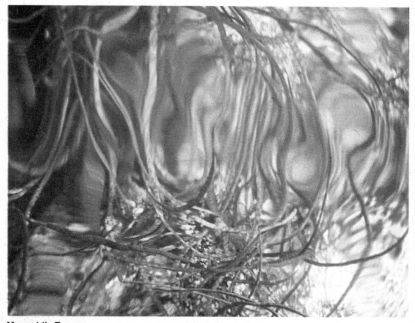

Mermaid's Tresses

thousand years the Chinese have been harvesting seaweed for food, and Confucius himself (551–497 BC) praised the curative values of the plant. Today seaweed is eaten in many oriental countries and in Japan accounts for 1 per cent of the country's total food intake. The three main types of seaweed used are: Nori, which is seaweeds of the *Porphyra* genus made into wafer-thin sheets of which millions are consumed each year; Kombu, which are hard greenish-black sheets, eaten raw, dried or cooked and are produced from laminarians; and Wakame, which is made from a dark green seaweed and is usually sold fresh, to be eaten in salads, soup, scrambled egg or sandwiches!

Seaweed is an extremely nutritious food because it has a fantastic ability to absorb nutrients from the sea and concentrate them in its tissues. Indeed its organic content is about 25 per cent protein, 45 per cent carbohydrate, 4 per cent fat, and a huge 26 per cent of other elements including most metals and vitamins. In Britain we have not completely ignored this nutritious source. Purple Lava *Porphyra umbilicalis* is still eaten in South Wales, particularly around Swansea, and also occasionally in North Devon. It can be boiled and mixed with lemon juice and eaten as a hot vegetable, as a salad, fried with bacon or used to make lava bread. This is prepared by washing the lava several times and boiling it until it is like an overcooked bowl of spinach, finally straining and forming it into flat cakes which are rolled with oatmeal and fried. These are typically eaten with eggs and bacon which, I am afraid, reduces the healthy aspect of the meal.

Green Lava *Ulva lactuca* is eaten raw with lemon juice as part of a salad where it resembles limp cabbage, and Dulse *Palmaria palmata* has been eaten raw in Scotland and Ireland and is said to be homeopathic. Carragheen or Irish Moss

Chondrus crispus is one of the most commonly used of our edible seaweeds. It is washed, bleached and dried to increase its flavour and can be made into blancmange or fruit jellies. During the Second World War Carragheen provided a valuable dietary supplement to the inhabitants of Jersey in the Channel Islands. Men were employed to gather and prepare the seaweed and to distribute it as a powder to the Island's chemists. When food was short, it was added to rabbit meat and said to be delicious. Personally I cannot see it being a familiar salad dressing in the pizza houses and hamburger take-aways of Europe, but in these days of anti-additive tendencies, and given the current vogue of healthy living, seaweed's nutritional properties have perhaps seen a new western renaissance. Of course it was the ancient Chinese who realised that kelp was effective as a cure for goitre, because of the iodine content of the weed, but Carragheen was later used in Ireland for the treatment of stomach ulcers, and in other countries was said to be a successful cure for intestinal ailments, blood disorders, dysentery, poor digestion, constipation, hay fever, nail disorders, hair loss, serious wounds, broken bones and so on. Once it was even claimed to be a useful protection against the hideous effects of radioactive fallout. I understand it grows particularly well on the coast around Sellafield!

Still, if not fit for us it is certainly fit for our food's foodstuff, and in Britain and most of Europe seaweed is commercially sold as an animal feed additive. In the past cattle refused to each such meal, but after it had been sweetened with sugar and its odour reduced they were found to produce higher than normal milk yields. Seaweed was in the past also harvested for fertiliser, and special rights for collecting drift seaweed and cutting living material were avidly guarded by groups of individuals who used this particularly in the potato growing areas of Scotland and Ireland. For many years a kelp industry thrived around the northern coast of France and the western coasts of Britain, whereby wracks and laminarian seaweeds were burned to produce alkaline ash which was used in the production of soap and glass. Later the industry suffered a boost when it was found that iodine occurred in the weeds. Today the seaweed industry is on the increase again and alginates, which can be recovered from many seaweeds, have many industrial applications in dairy products, puddings, fruit syrups, biscuit mixes and a host of other sweet sauces and dressings. Beer too has an alginate as a foam stabiliser. These substances also have a multitude of uses in the pharmaceutical industry, where they are used in the production of many tablets, powders, salts and even surgical threads and waxes for intricate operations. They also find their way into shaving cream, toothpaste, soap, shampoo, lipstick, air fresheners, photographic film, ceramic glazes, fireproofing fabrics, cocktail cherries, car carpeting and porcelain.

With these manifold uses it is not surprising that the cultivation of seaweed is also a developing industry. This has been pioneered by the Japanese who cultivate it in shallow bays where there is little wave action. Here they sow concrete paving stones on the sea floor, only to recover them a year later by which time they are engulfed in a thick growth of edible weed. In America, the Californian giant kelp, one of the world's fastest growing plants, is farmed on highly technical offshore platforms where between three and five hundred tonnes of seaweed are produced per acre annually. The Americans plan to extend these schemes by spending millions of dollars on huge offshore farming platforms. It appears that seaweed, that brown, smelly and boring stuff which gets stuck on the soles of your feet, causes you to slip head over heels into a rock-pool, or which children incessantly brandish or burst the bladders of, has a lot more to offer, not only to the seaside botanist, but possibly, in the future, also to the healthy living or starving hungry.

PLANTS VERSUS SALT

Oak and hazel woodlands are carpeted blue in May and spangled with pastel Primrose and dainty white Wood Anemones; dune slacks can be filled with the snowy covering of Wintergreens and Grass of Parnassus; in late August heathlands are brushed purple by a million million tiny heather blooms. In contrast our cliff-tops and sides generally have a spartan flora which is largely dependent on the adjacent countryside. Facing the brunt of the elements, the actual cliff-sides vary dramatically in terms of the vegetation which struggles to grow on them. On cliffs plant growth relies on the soil and organic debris, which collects in crevices and crannies, to root successfully. Cliffs which are almost sheer or made of hard rock, such as granite or basalt, have very few of these natural flower pots. Those made of softer rock are more easily eroded, their sides more transient and often the substrate never stable enough for any plants to grow successfully. Thus the cliff-side environment is, from a plant's point of view, one of the most inhospitable and harsh that it could choose to grow in. High winds or even light summer breezes make it difficult for young plants to get established. If the seeds are not actually dislodged by the wind, then the soil is perpetually dried by the sea-breeze, and for seedlings with shallow roots it is difficult to strain any vestige of water from the dusting of scant loamy or sandy soil. To overcome these problems many cliff-dwelling species are perennial, and have extensive root systems which anchor them firmly to the cliff, enabling them to withstand the gales and to reach deep down into the crevices where a little water may remain. Indeed, the drought conditions caused by the wind are not only a problem for seedlings, and many cliff plants have developed adaptations to conserve what little water remains. The leaves of some have been reduced to

LEFT **A rock flow**
RIGHT **Seahouse's seashore**

4. TENDER IS THE CLIFF

thin, needle-like structures, whilst others, such as Sea Beet *Beta vulgaris* ssp. *maritima* and Sea Campion *Silene vulgaris* ssp. *maritima*, have a thick waxy cuticle covering their leaves and stems which seals them against water loss. The stonecrops have developed swollen succulent leaves which hold a lot of water, enabling the plant to survive during any dry spells.

The most hostile and difficult cliff-side condition for a plant is, however, the high salinity. Sea water has a high osmotic pressure and an ionic mix far different from normal soils. If the osmotic pressure is higher outside than inside the plant, then the plant will lose water and dehydration will ensue. The few plants which survive in this habitat overcome this problem by increasing their internal pressure to a higher level than that of the external medium, by concentrating salt in their tissues. This prevents excessive water loss but creates another problem. Salt is potentially toxic to plants: some species have evolved special cells which can withstand a high salt concentration; others have developed organs such as salt glands, which secrete salt from leaves and roots in order to regulate their own salinity. Such salty secretions account for the pale frosty appearance of some cliff-side plants where excreted salt has remained on the leaf surface. Plants which tolerate such high levels of salt are known as halophytes.

On the lower parts of the beach where daily wave action racks the substrate it is impossible for any plant, salt-tolerant or not, to become established and this is the domain of the seaweeds. Above and along the drift line where disturbance is less frequent a sparse vegetation can brave the waves. Annuals such as Prickly Saltwort *Salsola kali*, Sea Rocket *Cakile maritima*, with its pretty pink flowers and succulent leaves, and Sea Mayweed *Matricaria maritima* can all endure salt spray, and root successfully in organic debris such as rotting seaweed. Here they are joined by Cleavers *Galium aparine*, Common Chick-

weed *Stellaria media* and Groundsel *Senecio vulgaris*. A characteristic feature of these species is that they can grow rapidly and seed quickly in the brief spells between the high tides and storms which continually annihilate these colonising species. Many can even increase their reproductive rate and output when salt concentrations build up in their tissues due to increased exposure to threatening waves or spray. This can be considered as a further adaptation enabling them to survive in this precarious habitat.

If there is a pebbly area further up the beach it may be stabilized by a thick carpet of Sea Campion. This species can tolerate frequent burial due to its combination of deep and aerial roots which will grow with renewed vigour, producing many new shoots, after any series of storms. Further back on the cliffs, beyond the reach of the highest tides, another set of halophytic species grows. Many of these are primarily salt-marsh plants such as Sea Plantain *Plantago maritima*, Common Sea-lavender *Limonium vulgare* and Thrift *Armeria maritima*. The latter grows in compact cushions which have evolved to protect the ground under the plant, by preventing soil erosion, and thus averting plant dehydration via its roots. These spongy, rounded clumps are obviously very successful in this respect as in May the entire cliff-top seems to be covered in pink icing, as thousands of pink blooms flicker in the breeze. Other species require more aerated soil and are therefore habitual cliff dwellers. These include Rock Samphire *Crithmum maritimum*, an umbelliferous species with leaves that are divided into long thick fleshy segments. Its yellow flowers appear between June and August. Joining the Samphire are the ancestors of our vegetables: Sea Beet, *Beta vulgaris* ssp. *maritima*, a straggling perennial which has small green flowers that appear in July; the Sea Radish *Raphanus raphanistrum* ssp. *maritimus*; the common

RIGHT **Cushions of campion**

Wild Cabbage *Brassica oleracea*, which has large expanded leaves; and others such as Fennel *Foeniculum vulgare*, Hoary Stock *Matthiola incana*, and Tree Mallow *Lavatera arborea*. On the steeper slopes chasmophytes or fissure plants struggle to grow in the sparse soils and shade of the rocks, whilst lichens encrust the bare and bleak rock-faces in marbled patterns of grey, green and yellow. The vegetation at the top of the cliff is influenced by the habitat immediately abutting the shelf, often moorland or grassland, but, like all of the species found clinging to the cliff-sides and shore, it is ultimately influenced by the soil and rock type.

Grazing by sheep and rabbits is always an important factor at the top of the cliff although these animals also seem to descend to ridiculously precipitous ledges to eat and here maintain a very short turf which is often dominated by the plantains. Sea Plantain, Buckshorn Plantain *Plantago coronopus* and Ribwort Plantain *P. lanceolata* grow in a sward less than a centimetre high along with a host of other grasses and grassland herbs. This type of short pasture is now becoming scarce and provides the ideal foraging habitat for one of Britain's least known and unusual birds.

CHOUGHS

Black and shiny, ever noisy and aerially adept, Choughs *Pyrrhocorax pyrrhocorax* are found along the west coast of the British Isles, the north west and south coast of Ireland, some areas of North Wales, Pembrokeshire and the western parts of Scotland. In Europe they can be found in Britanny, inland in the Alps, in Greece and Crete, but their greatest densities occur in the Iberian peninsula and Atlas Mountains. All across its range, the species has been gradually diminishing for the last two hundred years and it is now extinct on the English mainland.

Cornwall was their last bastion but the last time a pair bred there was in 1947, although a lone pair lingered there until 1967. This was a sad chapter in a continu-

Dorset foreshore

ous story of decline in the British population that occurred throughout the nineteenth century. However, this now seems to have been somewhat arrested. The last British census, performed in 1982, found a breeding population of about a thousand pairs supplemented by another 900 non-breeding birds. Most of these were spread around the Irish coastline, with only about 150 pairs breeding in Wales and on the Isle of Man. In Britanny only 35 pairs were found, which is an alarmingly low number, having further declined from the 40 pairs that frequented this area in 1973.

Choughs pair for life and can be seen together all year round. They are frequently gregarious and in Spain flocks of up to 200 may be seen together in July and August. In Britain the flocks normally range between 20 and 50, with the largest recorded being 231. In such numbers they are very conspicuous, spiralling and tumbling over the cliff-tops, with their free, elastic flight, forever calling with a distinctive high-pitched gull-like *Chweeaw* or *Chuff* which gives them their name.

The majority of our British Choughs nest on the coast, choosing sheltered openings in sheer rocky cliffs or ledges in coastal caves to lay their four creamy grey, blotched eggs. Their young are raised almost exclusively on a diet of insects and soil-living invertebrate larva such as leatherjackets, ants, beetles and spiders. These the adults extract using their slender, blood-red, curved bills to dig vigorously in short-cropped pasture. Holes about 5 centimetres deep are made in the turf where some ant species occur at densities of up to 15,000 per square metre. Not surprisingly such feeding areas are often revisited by gangs of foragers. Short maritime heathland or turf and short-grazed traditional rough pastures are prime Chough feeding grounds, and here they spend the majority of their foraging time. In winter they often scour the piles of seaweed blown in by storms, where they will find Sand Hoppers *Orchestia gammarella* and larvae of the Kelp Fly *Coelopa frigida* to their liking. Arable fields though, are rarely exploited; when Choughs are found inland it is in close association with sheep pasture: sheep-grazed land gives the closest cropped sward with the grass being only 1 to 3 centimetres high. Sheep dung also encourages dung beetles which seem to form part of all Choughs' diets.

Britain's population of 1,000 pairs is a significant proportion of the European population but because of its dependence on land used for livestock the Chough has suffered seriously through the modernisation of farming during the past two centuries. There has been a decline in sheep farming and inert arable fields have been pushed to within a few metres of the top of the cliffs in some places. Also the practice of fencing off the cliff-tops to prevent stray sheep from grazing these areas has reduced the amount of feeding space available for our Choughs. Increased tourist pressure, especially through the now numerous coastal paths, may in some places have caused prolonged disturbance. When all this is added together it seems that these factors have initiated an effective and rapid decrease in the number of breeding Choughs over the last two hundred years, whilst in more recent years egg collecting may also have led to further, isolated decline. Choughs are sedentary birds, so if a population is isolated inbreeding may well be a serious problem affecting recovery. Elsewhere in the world, Choughs are predominantly a montane species, dependent on short grasslands found at high altitudes, so their coastal nesting in Britain is a peculiar activity which was once perhaps encouraged by the grazing of livestock along our cliff-tops. They might have been most successful on the mild western coastlines because the climate here generally guarantees freedom from snow and frost which would bury or freeze their feeding grounds in winter. In any event it seems that to maintain the Chough in the present age will mean maintaining some farming methods from a bygone age. In these days of ravenous farming subsidies and general greed this is unlikely. I suspect that Choughs will achieve a tenuous yet tenable population level based on near natural factors and remain a comparatively rare species.

Shiny black, they can sometimes shine like silver, as the sun strikes their iridescent feathers against the dingy backdrop of the cliffs. Buoyant as foam in the air streams they bounce down to land on legs of blood-red to probe the plantains and plants that can stand the salty taste of the seaside. Catch them while you can.

Shoreline silhouette

SEABIRD SOCIAL ORDER

A deep blue sky hangs over the mild, May morning and despite the brilliant sharpness of the pointed sunlight the day is, as ever, chilled by a saline breeze. The sea is flat, lazy, dozing even, as you boat out to the giant iced bun which stands stark and ancient in the sea. Whether it is the Bass Rock, Ailsa Craig, Handa, St Kilda, or Sula Sgeir, it is a most spectacular, biologically important and exciting square kilometre for birdlife in Britain. This is truly bird-land. Forget the tricky tits on your garden bird-feeder, those pedestrian pigeons in the park, even geese raking in on wintery skeins or the waders of The Wash, because when it comes to our birds, nowhere will they dominate your senses with their sight, smell and sound more fully, nowhere are they more stimulating, more concentrated and more available than in the tremendous colonies which coat the islands that stud our western and northern shores.

From high over the top of the tower of bird-land to the lip of the sea, the air is jammed with swirling birds. Thousands of white, chocolate brown, black and grey feathers flex in the sunshine, the shades of the sheer stone planes. Here jammed on the precipitous cliffs, in a successful abuse of gravity, is a multitude of astounding proportions. Thousands, tens of thousands of braying birds. Skirting and puncturing your view are thousands more who flux 'twixt stone and shore, and revel in a continual cacophony of raucous shrieking akin to a primary school playground on carnival day. Such overcrowding results in all the expected squalor and hedonistic degeneracy. Bickering, stealing, fighting and an avian manifestation of all the deadly sins seem to dominate activities. Vain Gannets commit adultery, avaricious Guillemots covet their neighbours' ledges, rowing Razorbills are envious of the greedy Kittiwakes, whilst those foul and glutton-

LEFT **A Kittiwake tenement**
RIGHT **Lesser Black-backed Gulls**

A colony of Guillemots

ous Herring Gulls sloth about above this throbbing avian Tower of Babel. Stinking rubbish litters this city. A marvellous musty, ammonia-laden stench which rises to coat the cliff-top with a mixture of stale salt, rotten fish and guano. The smell is so strong it seems to paint your senses in 'eau de seaside'. Yet despite the apparent mayhem and clamouring chaos, there is within the colony a governing order both between and within each of the species' groups. Each of the rock-faces and slopes of the cliff is a specific microhabitat to which is attached a specific category of characteristic seabirds.

The lowest part, the bare rock zone, with its salt-splashed lichens and eroded fissures provides the main nesting areas for the shiny Shags *Phalacrocorax aristotelis* and dapper Black Guillemots *Cepphus grylle*. Behind this area any boulder scree or sheltered ledges hold Razorbill *Alca torda* nests. Such boulder fields can also be important for Puffins

Fratercula arctica, storm-petrels and shearwaters who excavate their breeding burrows in this honeycombed habitat. The middle and upper parts of the cliff, the most perilous and exposed section, is dominated by the true cliff-side aficionados. Here Guillemots *Uria aalge*, who can tolerate persistent physical contact with their neighbours achieve higher breeding densities than any other bird, whilst the dainty Kittiwakes *Rissa tridactyla* cement their fragile seaweed nests to the cliff with their copious dripping guano. Fulmars *Fulmarus glacialis* and Herring Gulls *Larus argentatus* are most typical of the upper cliff where bare rock becomes padded with grassy ledges and tufts of Thrift or Sea Campion and further up, on the cliff plateau, there is sufficient soil for Petrels, Shearwaters and Puffins to excavate their burrows. Herring Gulls, Great Black-backed Gulls *Larus marinus*, Lesser Black-backed Gulls *Larus fuscus* and the piratical skuas can also be found patrolling

Out of the storm

the air above the cliffs. It is though, impossible simply to classify the components of such a breeding bird community, because many other species such as Rock Dove, Jackdaw, Starling, House Sparrow, Chough, Black Redstart, Peregrine, Buzzard and Golden Eagle can join in this squawking, wheeling accumulation.

The British Isles are one of the world's outstanding seabird stations, and the enormous numbers of some species nesting here represent large proportions of the world's total population. Storm Petrels *Hydrobates pelagicus*, Gannets *Sula bassana*, Razorbills, Guillemots, Lesser Black-backed Gulls, Great Skuas *Stercorarius skua* and Manx Shearwaters *Puffinus puffinus* all have a significant proportion of their numbers based on British soil and many of these are concentrated into a very small number of sites. This is especially true of Gannets, Manx Shearwaters and the Storm Petrels. In fact the only seabird which is common all

around Britain's rocky coasts is that unsavoury cad – the Herring Gull.

Such a thronging of oceanic birds is possible because the path of the North Atlantic Drift, which with its warm and saline water, meets a zone of cooler, fresher, coastal water which lies over the continental shelf along the British and Irish coasts. Here, where the two water masses meet, the high marine productivity provides good feeding for fish and consequently for seabirds. Combine this with the geology of the north and west coasts of Britain, where hard, coarse-grained rocks erode to form helpfully horizontal ledges and indentations, and you have an almost ideal site for the resulting avian spectacular. My particular favourites are the sulas, the solans, the gantas, or more familiarly the Gannets.

THE GANNET
These ballistic bassanas bend in helicies across the front of the storm, side-slipping

like giant shearwaters, maybe four hundred miles from the gurgling roar of their colonies.

There are 17 British gannetries and they hold more than 70 per cent of the world's total population of Gannets. Stac an Armin and Stac Lee on St Kilda alone have more than 40 per cent of the total, with 65,000 pairs of these velvety sea geese.

Whether wheeling about offshore or at rest they are splendid birds, beautifully plumaged in a gossamer snow white and lustrous black. They have delicately painted bluish beaks punctuated by a neat round grey eye and heads washed with a tasteful coffee stain which fades out half way down their necks. The juveniles are of a mottled brown, which is gradually invaded with white from the bottom up, until they assume their adult plumage after four or five years.

The glamour and grace of the individual is entirely lost when these highly gregarious birds come together. They become a clammering, stinking gaggle, sprawling over the bare sands of their nesting grounds, decorated by Jackson Pollock guano. They are all insane and identical, stabbing viciously and precociously at any passing clone. They are so cruel, callous and calculating, so definitely selfish and scheming, each trying to cheat the other out of a centimetre of guano-stained sand, a scrap of smelly fish or a mate or an offspring. Yet despite this single-minded mess of brutality, the colony works and thrives. They attack and retreat, tease and appease, fight and flee to a strict code, continually outlined by means of a system of symbolic signals.

Gannets pair for life and forge such a strong relationship with a sensitive bill-tapping display, known as mutual fencing. The partners stand breast to breast with their wings out, shaking their heads from side to side, whilst gently knocking their bills together, and occasionally stretching their heads over and down the back of their mates. Whilst the dance continues, they utter, somewhat rudely, a deep and harsh *Urrah* call. This display may go on for a few minutes before both birds break into a routine of simultaneous and delicate preening of each other's neck and head. As this nuptial nibbling continues, the pair attempt to settle quietly in the colony. This is generally impossible because Gannets nest at a density of more than two pairs per square metre, and at such densities seem compelled continually to menace their neighbours and their neighbours' offspring. Each nest-site is a strictly defended territory. From the time the territory is re-established in January or February, at least one of the pair will be present to prevent any usurpers from immediately seizing the site, or robbing it of any precious nest material. When in attendance, adult males are particularly antagonistic and fighting is common. This can result in prolonged clashes with damaging results. The opposing combatants grip one another on their beaks or faces, twisting and jerking until their bill tips are forced under the rim of their opponent's eye or far down into its gaping mouth. Fortunately, throughout this affray there is little actual stabbing, although challengers may dive on opponents from the air and the pair of wrestling birds may continue fighting as they roll through the colony, over the edge of the cliff, and down into the sea. Such is the foul temper of an enraged Gannet. This aggression continues throughout the breeding season, even once pairs are well established and in the throes of rearing their single offspring. Incubated and brooded by both parents on a large compact pile of seaweed and feathers, cemented together by an unhealthy excretory glue, the youngster is fed twice daily by a partial regurgitation of fish such as Herring, Capelin, Cod, Coalfish, Pollock and Whiting. This the foraging adults catch with a dramatic plunge-diving technique, often as far as a hundred miles away from the colony.

These debauched Gannet gatherings are fantastically entertaining and a visit will leave an impression which persists long

The vanity of the Gannet

after the rich smell of the guano has faded from your splattered clothing. If you are careful and slow in your movements you can edge to within a few metres of the colony, and watch at exceptionally close range the antics of these most antagonistic and aggressive birds.

THE KITTIWAKE
Whilst the former fellows use the cliff plateau to breed, the delicate little Kittiwake selects the most perilous and precipitous parts of the cliff on which to plaster its nest. A true gull, and closely related to the Greater Black-backed, Lesser Black-backed and Herring Gulls which nest on top of the cliff, it shows a series of conspicuous adaptations to its change in life-style. Anatomically, it has longer toes and sharper claws, which help it grip on to the side of the cliff. Behaviourally, it shows only a meagre response to the appearance of a predatory Greater Black-backed Gull, since these birds pose little threat to the sheer-sided colonies of the Kittiwake. A colony of Black-headed Gulls, on sighting

such a predator, would respond *en masse* with a clamour of alarm calls, and prolonged and concerted mobbing. The Kittiwake's choice of the cliff-side habit also prevents these species, or foxes, from scrambling down to steal their eggs. Such security has allowed their response to predators to become reduced, and this in turn allows them more time to care for their young. It must be said however, that occasionally a rogue skua, Greater Black-backed Gull, or even a Gyrfalcon on the coasts of Norway, routs this ploy and plays havoc with a colony, preying upon most of its inhabitants. Such is the flavour of evolution.

Kittiwakes are not in the least fastidious about the cleanliness of their nest, as are their cliff-top cogeners, and it rapidly becomes stained with white flags of guano, and littered with discarded eggshells. Such tell-tale signals are an obvious clue to the whereabouts of the nest, easily spied by any hungry predator. Again, it is only their inaccessibility that saves them. Similarly, their chicks are not cryptically marked. They do exercise their growing wings remarkably less than other gulls, and spend most of their time sitting safely facing the cliff, motionless except for the turning of their heads. The youngsters also take food directly from the parent's bill, whereas the young of most other gull species pick it up after it has been regurgitated onto the ground. This adaptation prevents the eagerly awaited meal toppling into the sea or fouling the limited space around the nest-site. Breeding behaviour has also been modified, and many of the diverse range of displays performed by other gull species are condensed in the Kittiwake, tailored to function on the few square centimetres of ledge which form their territories. Consequently, Kittiwakes mate with the female sitting (whereas in other gulls she stands), so that the pair will not overbalance and topple off the ledge.

These ashy-blue screamers return to their colonies in March. The safest nest-sites are at the centre of the colony. These are usually seized by the oldest individuals and are fought over quite ferociously. Angry birds jab and peck at one another from their adjacent nest-sites, and sometimes engage in a bill-gripping tug of war. Occasionally both birds topple from the cliff-side and may even continue to fight in the sea, ducking each other's heads under the water. The less valuable sites at the edge of the colony are used by younger pairs.

As laying begins and while the eggs are being incubated the violence pales slightly and becomes more ritualised. Because of the bill's importance in aggressive displays and because there is so little space for contestants to back away on the cliff-sides, subordinates can frequently be seen tucking their bills into their neck- and breast-feathers as a show of submission and appeasement. This behaviour is seen, not only in adults who are arguing about nests, but also in the youngsters who may be bickering about a meal.

Adult Kittiwakes go foraging for nest material in groups of twenty or more, another unique facet of behaviour not seen in other gull species. This flock behaviour is probably an anti-predatory adaptation, because away from their cliff-side haunts Kittiwakes are on unfamiliar ground. Both sexes help collect a mass of mud, grass and seaweed which they compact, by trampling and smoothing with their breasts and tails, into a carefully made bowl which holds their two or three greyish eggs. Throughout May the brightly coloured adults incubate these, continually irritating one another with their sulphur yellow bills, blood-red mouths and stiff-winged antics until the eggs hatch in early April. The Kittiwake may be the loveliest gull, but it is not the most striking, or popular, of the seabirds.

THE PUFFIN

Parrotesque with their yellow, red and orange bills, velvety shirts and glossy black backs Puffins bullet off their ramparts and whirr down to the sea at speeds of 80 kilometres an hour; surprisingly fast for a small bird which has had its wings

P-P-P-Puffin

clipped, in a compromise between airborne ability and the need for underwater propulsion. Nevertheless, with wings beating at three or four hundred strokes a minute, they power back from the sea, running the gauntlet of the kleptoparasitic intentions of Greater Black-backed Gulls who loiter over the colony. The bills of the returning Puffins are crammed full of Sand Eels and Sprats for their ugly, underground progeny and at times the Puffin colony, which is dug like a rabbit warren into a bed of hummocky soil, is a gyrating honey-pot of activity, with Puffins circling continually over the burrows in what is termed a 'wheel'.

This madcap milling of birds is thought to be an anti-predator strategy, because the poor adult Puffins are often preyed upon by Greater Black-backed Gulls. The gulls hang over the colony in the updraughts, occasionally swooping at perched Puffins, if their patience runs out, in a bid to panic them into flight. Once in the air single Puffins are selected by the gulls, who pursue them from above and behind, presumably seeking advantage from the Puffin's blind spot. If the Puffin sees the gull, it takes a terrified tumble into the sea and the gull will let it escape. But if it makes no response, the gull soon seizes its much smaller prey, and drags it struggling to a flat area of rocks or grass, where it is stabbed to death by the gull's heavy yellow bill. Once the Puffin is killed the entrails and breast muscles are eaten, the skin is turned inside out and the bones picked clean, before the skull is cleaned out and the head swallowed whole, to be later regurgitated as a pellet.

The horror this may induce in some people should be constrained however, because this is a natural predation process and in fact man is still the most serious predatory threat that the world's Puffins face. For thousands of years human coastal communities have exploited large numbers of seabirds to supplement their diet and desire for delicacies. In the past Puffins' eggs were dug from their burrows,

The Farne's Cliffs

the young were extracted or exhumed using pointed sticks, specially bred dogs were used to harvest young Puffins leaving their burrows and huge nets were thrown over colonies to catch hundreds of birds in a single session. More recently Puffins were systematically shot during the breeding season. Of course all of these activities had a detrimental effect on the population, yet harvesting of these birds continues in some form in several parts of their range. In the Faroes (a tiny group of windswept islands between Scotland and Iceland) bird fowling, or fleyging, still continues and contributes many tonnes of useful meat each year. Most of the Puffins are caught in July, using a large triangular net fastened to a pair of wooden supports which are lashed to a three or four metre long pole. This gadget is called a fleygastong, and is held with one hand near the bottom of the pole and the other much higher up, so that the net can be easily levered into the air to overtake any hesitating Puffin which is attempting to alight amongst a series of decoys set on the cliff-top. Fleyging sites are traditional, some having been used for hundreds of years, and when a moderate wind blows along the cliff, stimulating many immature Puffins to visit, up to 900 birds can be caught in a single day. The catch is carried away tucked into waistbands, tied to headbands or in such huge volumes that ponies are called in to take them back to a team of women who pluck two or three hundred each a day. After plucking the trussed corpses are frozen and sold in supermarkets. The meat on these birds is dark and not at all fishy tasting, and is prepared by stuffing with a rich cake mixture and roasting, although in Iceland and Norway Puffins are also boiled, smoked or salted for consumption. Happily Puffins today are protected during the breeding season in every country except the Faroes and Iceland, where catches of perhaps 20,000 and 200,000 respectively are still made each summer. In Britain they are thriving at their larger colonies and provide an entertaining diversion for fair weather birdwatchers. But I am afraid that in the spectacle stakes they are far surpassed in their sleep, because a visit to one of our Manx Shearwater colonies on a moonless or cloudy night has to be one of any naturalist's lifelong superlatives.

SHEARWATERS AND PETRELS

It was two o'clock in the morning, and I had been awakened by the eerie wailings which wheeled overhead. I emerged from the comfort of a chalet on Scomer, a tiny island off the Welsh coast. Using my torch like a Starwars light-sabre, I sent columns of light up through the scant mist to illuminate these lunatics, straffing them for a few seconds as they careered over the island, about three or four metres above the damp morass of bracken. They croon, crow and coo continually to locate their mates, whose nesting burrows are hidden in the crumbling honeycomb of sandy turf. And once inside the burrows they indulge in a raucous duet of staccato cackling. I soon discovered one of these birds at my feet uninjured yet totally crippled by its temporary grounding, unable even to scurry away properly. The bird was easy to capture, and examination revealed long, stiff, blade-like wings, a smooth, almost waxy, sleek and sinuous body and stupidly short legs serving to define it as a transparently airborne lifeform. Consequently on the

ground they appear embarrassed by their predicament as they try to shuffle away into their burrows before you can stretch on your knees to grab them. I wondered how on earth these birds would manage to get into the air again, and concluded that they must have to waddle to the edge of the cliffs and throw themselves over in order to gain enough momentum for flight. I learned much later that, although this technique is common practice for the fledging young, the adults use their beaks and wings to clamber up well channelled grooves in the many low boulders which cover the island, and using these as take-off platforms regain their composure by dropping back into flight.

In the few hours of darkness thousands of these birds swarm in to find their nests, feed their partners or progeny and then dissolve out to the safety of the sea for the daytime, free from the perils of the many marauding Lesser Black-backed Gulls which would easily pick off these inept land travellers in daylight. The largest British population of Manx Shearwaters *Puffinus puffinus* is on Rhum, in the north western isles of Scotland, where an estimated 135,000 pairs have burrows. These are occupied between February and September and both sexes incubate and care for the single offspring which is eventually abandoned after 60 days of a diet of small fish, crustaceans and surface-floating offal. This, it seems, is enough to prepare the chick for the perils of its first fall or flight over the cliff-side and a journey which takes them across the Atlantic to the coast of South America for the winter.

Closely related to the Manx Shearwater is the tiny bat-like Storm Petrel *Hydrobates pelagicus*. This sooty black bird has a white rump patch, a squarish tail and black feet, which serve to distinguish it from the rarer fork-tailed Leach's Petrel *Oceanodroma leucorhoa*. While on a visit to Scomer, I was fortunate enough to discover a small number of these birds breeding in a tumble of boulder scree and, while I cowered amongst the rocks, the tiny

Manx Shearwater out of its element

home-coming petrels brushed my face like lacy, black butterflies. More amazing than startling, they repeated this caress as they tried to locate their purring partners hidden inside their secret, summer, breeding chambers. These hollows seem to amplify the harsh, sustained and penetrating *Arrr-r-r-r-r-r* call, which can sometimes drone on for several hours, only occasionally being punctuated with an abrupt and hiccoughing *Chikka*. This song is produced by a lonely bird awaiting the return of its partner, and serves to advertise the occupation of the burrows to other adult petrels. Pairs have been seen performing gentle aerial chases above their breeding burrows in May and June, but the breeding

antics of these magical little birds are almost completely unknown, because any attempt to observe them with white light frightens them. They also move too quickly and erratically to follow with a torch beam, so I had only mystical views while laying staring at the stars at the base of their burrows, until they flapped over the warmth of my rising breath. Such nocturnal encounters with both petrels and shearwaters may be romantic, but they can give a very poor impression of the bird's potential. Both of these tube-nosed birds are really species of the open ocean and it is only here that their skill at surfing, slanting and skewing amongst the hummocks of the sea can be fully appreciated.

PEREGRINES

It was dawn on a day in midsummer when I pulled my way out of the sleeping compartment of my Renault 5. (I know these cars do not have sleeping compartments. I know it very well.) I crossed some stiles and old stone walls and trod the short turf to the top of the cliffs. Here, like bonfire ash blowing in the wind, Jackdaws jigged and jerked, black in the grey scape. They barked and rolled about like a gang of lads out on a Friday night, buoyant and joyous in the buffeting currents. I watched these charcoal kites for a moment and thought that if I were to be reborn in animate form I would like to be one of those Jackdaws on the South Wales coast.

The Jackdaws dropped out of sight through the pink bubbles of thrift which carpeted the cliff-top, smooth, waxy and green. Their globular flower heads vibrated incessantly and despite their simplicity of form, *en masse* their pinkish sheen added a pretty pastel shade to the otherwise green- and blue-dominated view. A last Jackdaw spun up from the sea and careered away westerly in the draught. As I found him with my binoculars the wind licked his lazy wings for a second or two, but then suddenly he took control of nature. He turned, plummeted, and I lowered my binoculars just in time to see him vanish magically through the cliff-top into the deep, craggy cove below.

I carefully made my way to the edge of the cliff through the slippery hummocks of thrift and Bladder Campion until the inlet lay like a giant bowl before me. Way below the tame sea slapped the yellow crusted boulders, and a few Kittiwakes 'kittiwaked' across the shore. A single Herring Gull racked the scene with its usual acoustic abuse. The whole scale of the place was enormous. It took me a full five minutes to locate my idol and her family, hidden in the contrasty shade of a twenty ton overhang of rock. The princess of Pembroke was, as

LEFT **Home of the Peregrine**
RIGHT **Herring Gull**

ever, beautiful. For me Peregrine Falcons *Falco peregrinus* are one good reason to put up with any hardship. They are always exciting, entertaining and worthy of however long a trip is needed to see them. Today, fortunately, they are also much more common, and they can be found along much of Britain's western coastline.

At rest this Welsh falcon was a round, innocuous feathery toy with big black eyes. She was bothered by the flies which played over some neglected carrion, and occasionally she would flick her listless wings in a vain attempt to dissuade these insects from coming too close. Not hungry, she was unprimed, relaxed, dangerless. Alongside her were two young Peregrines, or eyases, wriggling and scraping in their downy drowse. Then the sun punctured through the clouds and struck the black-blueness of her back. She preened for a few seconds before striding out into the air. In a second she had transformed from a toy into a supple, sprung weapon with wings like scythes of slate. If animals do not feel pleasure why was this bird rolling and flaunting so joyously! Again and again, she would slide over the cove, with flickering wings. Then gliding, then slamming the sky and thundering away in a searing slide across the cove. She turned on an uplift of air and produced a pretty, delicate, chattering trill which belied her intention to kill. She then slipped sideways around the edge of the cove and disappeared.

For perhaps a half an hour I peered nosily at the eyases, before their lethargy infected me and I fell asleep on the soft cushions of the cliff-top vegetation in the early morning sunshine. I awoke 50 minutes later feeling as fresh as I had when I'd first closed my eyes. There was no dryness in my mouth or eyes and no thirst which such careless collapses to unconsciousness can sometimes produce in less healthy surroundings. In my absence the falcon had returned to a ledge adjacent to that of her nest-site, and there she was waddling about like a dancing duckling. Beneath her was the corpse of a freshly

killed Feral Pigeon in Rock Dove disguise. She had already opened the breast of her prey, but now returning to it she pinned it down with her huge talons and began to peel off thin strips of muscle. I watched the princess until late afternoon, by which time I had established that she was supporting a family of three. Just before I left, the male falcon, or tiercel, limped across the cove and in a frenzy of excited twittering left a corpse of one of those careless lads, the Jackdaws. I made an instant decision that should I be reborn I would after all be one of these Pembrokeshire Peregrines and not one of those lazy corvids.

Pigeons and Jackdaws have in the past been cited as the coastal Peregrine's favourite prey. Because this predator is so widely distributed, not only in our own islands but throughout the rest of the world, it is not surprising that it is a more catholic feeder than this. It usually draws its prey from the part of the bird fauna which is most abundant in the environment it is frequenting. If there are major colonies of cliff-nesting birds, such as Guillemots, Razorbills, or Puffins, these will form a large proportion of the Peregrine's diet. If there is an estuary nearby then Redshank, Oystercatcher, Ringed Plover, Teal, Widgeon and the gull species will also be included. If the cliff-tops are scoured by the falcons then birds as small as Meadow Pipits, Wheatears, Stonechats and Skylarks will find their way onto the Peregrine's plucking post. There are also many reports of unusual prey being killed. All five species of British owl have been predated, and Peregrines have been flushed from the carcasses of Arctic and Long-tailed Skuas, Sparrowhawks, Kestrels, Buzzards and even other Peregrines. House Martins, Swifts and Swallows are also occasionally taken, particularly by male Peregrines who can apparently seize these poor fellows from the air with unbelievable ease.

RIGHT **The Princess of Pembroke – the toy . . .**

A Peregrine family needs 225 kilograms of prey a year in order to survive and rear two youngsters. Consequently, Peregrines constitute a serious threat to any other avian inhabitants of the shore. Occasionally, however, they become very specialist feeders, preying almost exclusively on a single species, and unfortunately Pigeons are often a favourite for this abuse. Indeed, in the past they were persecuted by pigeon fanciers, and in the last war Peregrines were pronounced by HM Government as the original spycatchers, when they were thought to be intercepting message-carrying homing pigeons. They were persecuted in a systematic fashion, not unlike ex-members of the secret services, resulting in local depletion.

Peregrines, being such cosmopolitan feeders, require only the bare essentials of open country, over which to hunt, and steep rock-faces, for nesting-sites. Consequently, there are few parts of Britain which cannot support them for at least some part of the year. In fact in winter Peregrines can appear almost anywhere. In the summer their cliff-nesting requirement confines them to the more precipitous parts of our coastline, or to mountains and moorlands inland. In the past Peregrines regularly bred all around the British coast where there were cliffs of more than 30 metres in height, and were really only absent from the coastal section

... the weapon

CATCHER IN THE SKY

of eastern England which runs from Kent to the south of Yorkshire. In the halcyon days before the pesticides scandal and the pressure of people penalised our Peregrines, they could be seen on the cliffs above Dover harbour, on the outskirts of holiday resorts all along the south coast and on the chalky slopes of the Isle of Wight. Further north they were perfectly at peace on the basalt precipices of the Hebrides, the flagstone walls of red sandstone in Caithness and Orkney and on the wild granite and chalk of our western shores. Today, in our over-populated land, the Peregrines prefer to nest on inaccessible and formidable precipices, resulting in it being a predominantly coastal species in many parts of its range. Peregrines always show a distinct preference for ledges used before, some nest-sites probably having been used for hundreds of years. The ledges selected need to be big enough to hold a full brood of four large, bickering young. Although Peregrines do not build their own nests, they will occasionally scratch out a shallow bowl in the soil with their feet or very frequently take over the disused nest of another cliff-nesting bird. These requisitioned nests are much sought after, particularly those of Ravens which often have their wool lining removed before the falcon lays her eggs. Less often eyries of Golden Eagles or Buzzards, or nests of Carrion Crows, Jackdaws, Herring Gulls or, very rarely, Cormorants and Shags are utilised. This cliff-nesting habit is of course an adaptation against predation, and the suitability of the nest ledge depends largely on its inaccessibility. Nest-sites usually have a large overhang of rock above and below, providing protection from falling rocks or ice, as well as predators. During winter these storm-blown and inhospitable crags may be deserted by the Peregrines, who flee to the bird-filled estuaries and low-lands. Here they normally appear to be solitary, but occasionally birds may be in a pair for the winter period. Courtship may begin during autumn and extend through the winter until

the beginning of the breeding season. By late February one or more of the pair returns to their nesting-site, males usually arriving first and females often returning to the site where they nested the previous year. During the first two weeks of March any unmated males may attempt to lure females to their cliff by parading between their suitable nesting ledges and uttering a wailing 'witchewing', akin to a rusty gate. The males also indulge in spectacular aerial courtship flights. During these manic manoeuvres they plunge up and down, roll over and over and dart about the cliff, often soaring in tight circles. At other times the female may also join in this melée and the birds will chase and stoop at one another in a dazzling dog fight, pulsing apart over the cliff-tops and then plummeting together in an extraordinary aerial game of 'tag'. Occasionally during these manoeuvres the birds may close together, chest to chest, and indulge in talon grappling. On two occasions Peregrines have even been seen to engage their beaks in flight. Surely one of nature's most extraordinary and exciting kisses.

By the beginning of April, after periods of courtship feeding and a variety of cliff-side displays, which involve males and females bobbing, dancing, 'wickering' and 'whinneying' on the fresh, spring, salt air, the birds copulate and produce a clutch of three or four red-brown freckled, mottled and blotched eggs. These are incubated, primarily by the female, for about 33 days. During this time both parents protect their nest-site and if inflicted with any human disturbance they will fly up and circle around the nesting cliff giving a cackling alarm call. This commotion attracts the missing member of the pair, and continues until any intruder leaves the area.

It takes between 50 and 55 hours for the Peregrine chicks to struggle out of their eggs into the May sunshine and the tumultuous aura of activity which has by then enveloped the cliff-side. These youngsters can stand upright by about 22 days and after 25 days are feeding for themselves.

55

But it is a full 40 days before the young Peregrine takes his first fragile flight out over the sea, usually ending in a clumsy crash landing and an extraordinarily senseless chorus of screams from many thousands of seabirds who share the cliff-side habitat. It is as if they know what this untidy package of predator will some day turn into.

THE SKUAS

If the Peregrine is nature's ultimate winged assassin, it has a serious pretender to the throne in the form of those supple, thieving devils – the skuas. These fierce birds are related to gulls, but are all dark coloured and distinguished by their long, narrow pointed wings, robust bodies and long tails. The Arctic *Stercorarius parasiticus* and Great Skuas *S. skua* nest in Britain, whilst the Long-tailed *S. longicaudas* and Pomarine Skua *S. pomarinus* visit during autumn, when they chase and cheat Terns all the way down the coast of Europe, North Africa and out to the Patagonian seas off Argentina. At this time you can watch them dashing along the strand line, or just offshore, like crazy broken-winged falcons, flexing, stalling and somersaulting in an acrobatic freestyle flight. Usually they kleptoparasitise Terns, meaning they harry them until they drop their food which the Skuas steal, but this technique is also used against just about every other seabird. Arctic Skuas can be between 50 and 80 per cent successful in these endeavours and the noisy chases usually last between 8 and 15 seconds before the smaller victim is scared out of its bird-brain and drops its Sand Eel or Sprat, which the skua may seize even before it hits the water. When Fulmars are abused this raucous game of tag can last for as long as 3 minutes, before they finally concede and regurgitate their booty. Either way, the skua's persistence is admirable, as it twists and turns, bends and spins as if it is joined to the fleeing victim. When chases occur in high winds the birds appear speeded up and it becomes a manic spectacle.

Nevertheless, Skuas are notoriously unpopular; even modern conservationists give them a fairly villainous appraisal. Their piratical feeding reputation is further depreciated by their habit of raiding other seabirds' nests of eggs or young, and by the belligerent brutality sometimes displayed by that bully of bullies the Bonxie, or Great Skua. This Herring-Gull-sized brute is an overweight brother of the Arctic Skua, from whom it can be distinguished by its bulky, barrel-shaped body and broad, more-rounded wings. Its interest in food piracy is reduced in the breeding season when, using its increased power, it is a fierce predator of seabirds and their off-spring. This practice sometimes leads to grisly scenes of Puffin tug of war between a pair of greedy Skuas. However such anarchic antics are not really that common, because fish gathered from behind boats or dipping into surface shoals or, I admit, piracy, are still the main source of food. The problem lies in the fact that this is a species which occasionally throws up rogue individuals who continually predate the same source, and in the past this has included weak lambs. Of course such habits are exaggerated by folklore and unfortunately Skuas of both species are still illegally shot by shepherds when they return to their breeding grounds in spring. At this time their reputation is not enhanced by their incredible aggression at the nest. Sheepdogs are driven back by continual beatings, and even human intruders can be badly injured by these screaming Skuas' feet. These are unique in that they are the only webbed birds' feet to be armed with predatory claws, all the better to grip, rip and scratch you with.

To me all this rip-roaring speed and swash-buckling piracy are superb, and the sight of a cinnamon streak shearing out of the sun to clout you amounts to jolly good fun, but then I suppose I am not a Tern with chicks to rear, or a tired Puffin who just wants to rest in his burrow.

RIGHT **Puffin**

OTTERS

It would have been nice to include Otters *Lutra lutra* in a book about quiet, inland streams with a description of dappled willow trees set in lush, lowland meadows, a slow, heavy river full of Chubb, Rudd and Dace, and an Otter frolicking in the dusky orange sunlight. Today, such visions are victims of nostalgia because although a few Otters remain on southern streams they are almost impossible to see due to their nocturnal habits. Now it is only in the north-west Western Isles of Scotland that you can glimpse these marine mustelids with any regularity in daylight.

While on a photographic foray in the outer Hebrides some friends of mine were fortunate enough to have superb views of an Otter feeding in a sea loch. Seemingly unconcerned by their presence, this animal returned, with crabs to devour in front of its dribbling audience, to a small slab of seaweed-encrusted rock some 30 metres offshore. They ogled this otter for two hours in glorious sunlight, before it eventually swam off across the loch and out towards the open sea. Later their ecstatic descriptions were punctuated by irritating recollections of how clearly they could see its long whiskers, or vibrissae, which it uses to find food in murky water. Whilst this splendid show was on, I, at the beginning of my photographic career, had spent two hours photographing a pair of dead moths in a stream!

For most modern naturalists, finding an Otter is like coming across the Holy Grail at a jumble sale. It is one of the ultimate prizes, a kind of dreamed of jewel, which will take pride of place in the cerebral crown of wild memories. For Terry Nutkins though it used to be an everyday event, sometimes an every-minute event, and even though a rather angry Otter tore two of his fingers off, they have never lost their appeal in his crammed life with animals.

LEFT **A wet Otter**
RIGHT **Otter country**

Razorbills

Terry is one of the last wilderness boys. He spent his early teens on the west coast of Scotland, living with Gavin 'Ring of Bright Water' Maxwell in a windswept cottage called Camusfearna. During the long winter nights Terry otterised with Teko, whom he reared, Edal, who bit his fingers off, and two wild Otters who lived under the floor boards. He walked them like dogs, caught fish for them, nurtured them and played with them for hours on end. Although Edal and Teko were much larger African Otters, their habits and behaviour are similar to the European species. Terry's intimate contact, fused during his stranded teens, was further fuelled by a period as a prawn fisherman on Skye, when each day he saw Otters playing on the foreshore by his house. He knows as if by magic their intentions or moods; perhaps it is a twinkle in their eye, the angle of their ears, or a tiny whinneying under their breath, that is the signal. More likely it comes from a memory of an Otter playing

with a torch beam on his bedroom floor, thinking it was solid and caressing it with its curling tail as it might a slippery fish, while Terry giggled and smiled in the lamp light of one of the loneliest homes in the world.

For the full story, including the tale of two fingers, read Maxwell's 'The Rocks Remain', a sequel to the 60s smash 'Ring of Bright Water'. I read the latter in about 1969, aged eight. I re-read it every night. I still remember every photograph of Mijbil, the star; I did projects at school, saw the film, four times, and played Val Doonican's theme music to death on the crackly old record player. All with no hope of seeing a real Otter near my south coast home. In a genuine, and probably desperate, attempt to satiate my obsession my Mother made what can only be described as the most hideous, deranged, malformed and tawdry toy otter. Fashioned from nylon fur pile, with a tube for a body and two green inverted button eyes, not even curling it up at night, illuminating it with a torch and squinting at it could make it look like an Otter. Years later, Terry and I recall this contrast hysterically and marvel at how our ottery and otterless lives finally collided in a great friendship.

However, since my tortured teens I have ottered, albeit with a captive pair playing in a tank which permitted views of them underwater. They were bending and bow-breaking, slipping, rolling, squeezing through the green of the algae-covered pond, like a pair of twisting eel-metal torpedoes. They exploded through the silvery, foaming surface, causing an energetic fission and fusion of tiny spherical bubbles, like a mad, underwater firework, whilst their fish food flashed amber and flinched about in the deadlight areas at the bottom of their tank. On land the Otters transformed into terrestrial animals; at first smooth, but once they had shaken themselves their fur was spiky bright. They chased around their lawn, so bright, so energetic, so engulfed by the joy of life.

In the past, Otters were heavily persecuted by bailiffs and other people involved in the care of game fishing interests, because of the damage they were said to do to salmon stocks. In fact they catch fish in an inverse proportion to their ability to escape, the bigger the fish the more likely it is to escape and the less Otters will chase it, and so if salmon are taken they are usually only very small specimens. But, fish of some kind do constitute a vast proportion of their diet, although crustaceans, aquatic insects, birds and mammals may occasionally be caught along the bank, in the mud and under stones. Once located, their prey is seized in their mouths. Their front paws are only used to manipulate it while they chew and bite their way through the scales or shell of their lunch. In captivity Otters may live up to 20 years, and during this time they breed every year, at any time of the year. The female produces two or three young in a litter which is initially cared for by her in the nest, or holt. The rearing process is a long one and cubs may still be suckling after 10 weeks, when they first enter the water.

Any enthusing about the Otter's aquatic ability pales before that observed in the seals, because the feathery footed Pinnipedia are perhaps the most superior mammalian adaptation to life in water, while still holding a tenuous flipper hold on the land. Only the cetaceans (whales and dolphins), who have abandoned any vestige of life on land, are better adapted to the submarine life.

SEALS AND WHALES

A seal's limb bones are short and almost completely withdrawn into the bulk of the body, leaving only the slippery flippers protruding. The digits of these are connected by a webbed skin, to increase the surface area of this paddle. As well as bringing the source of power nearer the body, the lack of any long ungainly terrestrial type of limb means that the animal is far more streamlined, and streamlining here is in the superlative form. The head is smooth and rounded, lacking any long external ears and passes, without an apparent neck, into the trunk. This may be plump, rounded, sinuous or elongated, but it tapers and ends in a small tail which fits neatly behind the hind flippers. Of course these submersible adaptations present problems when the seals come ashore to rest or breed and because their flippers cannot support the body weight seals move by wriggling or sliding. On land they thus appear stranded, uncomfortable, ungainly and ugly, like unfinished plasticine models which a careless child has deprived of legs. But in the water chalk becomes cheese and they penetrate the liquid like graceful marine missiles, able to dive or rise, start or stop with effortless ease.

Several important adaptations are involved in the seal's ability to dive. Firstly, they keep water out of their lungs by sealing their nostrils, using a plug of cartilage squeezed into the breathing tube by the moustachial pad. Secondly, they manage to overcome the 'bends' phenomenon by breathing out slightly as they dive, to reduce the amount of air in their lungs. They thus greatly reduce the volume of nitrogen which comes out of the blood and into the body tissues during the dive. This dissolved gas would turn into free gas on re-surfacing and the resulting bubbles would cripple or kill any mammal. Thirdly, in seals the immediate response to submersion is an amazing slowing down of the heart rate, a reaction known as bradycardia. This conserves oxygen in the blood which is further enhanced by constricting most of the peripheral blood vessels so that only the essential organs, such as the brain, are supplied with the all essential oxygen. To further prolong diving, seals also have an extraordinarily large volume of blood, as much as three quarters more than a man of similar weight, and the ability to store large volumes of extra oxygen in their muscle tissue. All these adaptations permit seals to remain active in the pursuit of their prey long after breathless human divers would have been cramped, drowned, or got the bends. Once they return to the surface a period of high speed beating of the heart, or tachycardia persists for up to 10 minutes while all the oxygen that has been used in the muscles is replaced.

The Grey Seal *Halichoerus grypus*, Britain's rocky shore species, is fond of catching Flounders, Whiting, Herring and salmon, for which it sometimes has a preference, during its dives. Stealing from salmon nets has given this Roman-nosed raider a bad name, and they are frequently shot at the nets and culled at their breeding grounds. This has had little effect on their population and now another problem has transpired. These seals are the intermediate host for Codworm *Terranova decipiens*, a nematode which is becoming increasingly abundant in our cod catches. Once cooked this presents no problem to humans, but selling wormy fish does pose a problem to the fishermen, so the seals retain their unpopularity, even though the

Scottish salmon stocks have been annihilated by our over-fishing and not that of these dusky-toned divers. But accomplished divers though seals are, when it comes to deep or prolonged diving the true experts are the dolphins and whales.

These animals have the ability to squash their lungs and hold any oxygen they take with them on a deep dive in the non-absorbtive chambers of the windpipe and their nasal passages. Again this reduces the amount of nitrogen dissolving in the body tissue and later prevents the bends when ascending to the surface. Also the entire respiratory surface of cetaceans is covered with fine capillaries, so that any stray nitrogen that does escape into the body is rapidly returned to the lungs, when back on the surface. Both of these acute adaptations allow some of the larger whales to descend to over 3,000 metres and remain under water for up to 2 hours without coming up to breathe. Down in these dark depths these krakens are feeding on fish, squid, krill or plankton, but how do they find their prey?

The smell, taste and eyesight of cetaceans is notably poor, and it is hearing or echo location that is their most developed sense. In the dolphins, the melon, a waxy, lens-shaped body set in their forehead, focuses sounds produced in the nasal passages into a narrow beam of ultrasonic pulses. These clicks and whistles are returned to the animal through oil-filled passages in the lower jaw and finally to the inner ear. This highly sensitive organ is isolated from the skull by means of a bubbly foam which reduces interference from any extraneous resonances and allows them to build up an incredibly fine picture of their surroundings. Similar apparatus is found in whales, who produce an eerie synthesis of pulsed clicks, whines and whistles to communicate through miles and tonnes of the oceans which they once thrived in. Indeed whales are very much offshore animals and of all the whales of the north east Atlantic it is only the Minke Whale *Balaenoptera acutorostrata* that is likely to be seen from the British headlands during the summer months. Many smaller dolphins seem to move inshore at this time and the White-beaked *Lagenorhynchus albirostris* and Common Dolphins *Delphinus delphis* are those most often seen bouncing about off our western shores. If you are lucky enough to spot a cetacean from some jagged promotory at all it is almost sure to be a Common Porpoise *Phocoena phocoena*, which will appear as a fat, black barrel which you could have sworn was there a second ago. You point at an unmarked wave.

Your friend bleats 'Where, where?'
'There.'
'Where?'
'Just near where that gull is . . . now!'

Nothing. He or she sees a gannet and turns away and the sea pig rolls over.
'There.'
'Where?'

So it begins again until you have both stood staring dizzily at the sea for 20 minutes and the porpoise is long gone.
'Well it was there.'

And so we conclude this squint at the life of rocky shores. From that shy animal, the limpet, to the highly re-evolved porpoise all the flora and fauna here has been welded into a compromise between the three states of matter. The sea, land and sky of the shore has limited and directed an extraordinary evolution of forms which would take a lifetime to admire. Do not waste any time.

The Roman-nosed Grey Seal

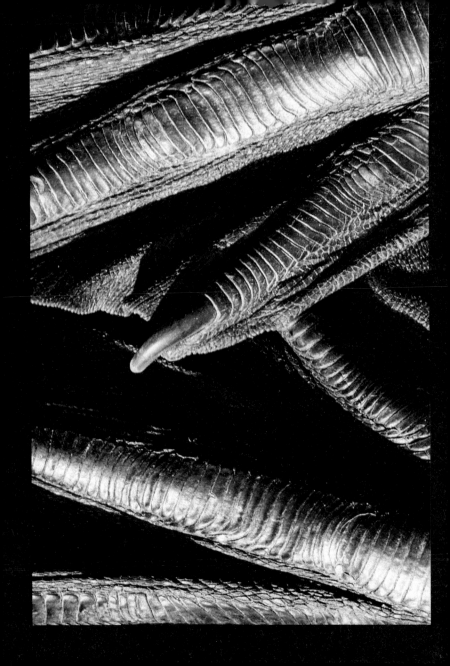

Identification of what is around you will greatly increase your enjoyment of Natural History. The following pages describe the species that are most likely to be encountered in a Rocky Shore habitat. Each species is also featured in a colour plate, representative of the type of habitat in which it is most likely to be found. The combination of the picture and description should enable you to find out what is flying, standing, buzzing or growing in front of you. Unless otherwise stated all the measurements given are, in the case of plants, heights or, in the case of animals, lengths.

Rocky Shoreland Residents–A GUIDE

LEFT **The reptilian Cormorant**
RIGHT **A Scaup**

ROCK POOL

1 Eider (p. 86)
2 Turnstone (p. 95)
3 Ringed Plover (p. 95)
4 Spiny Starfish (p. 83)
5 Common Starfish (p. 83)
6 Common Limpet (p. 81)
7 Shore Crab (p. 82)
8 Dog Whelk (p. 81)
9 Common Prawn (p. 82)
10 Assymetric Barnacle
11 Common Acorn Barnacle (p. 81)
12 Common Sea Urchin (p. 83)
13 Rock Goby (p. 83)
14 Butterfish (p. 84)
15 Lumpsucker (p. 83)
16 Sea Lemon (p. 81)
17 Blue-rayed Limpet (p. 80)
18 Beadlet Anemone (p. 80)
19 Father Lasher (p. 83)
20 Snakelocks Anemone (p. 80)
21 Velvet Crab (p. 82)
22 Common Mussel (p. 81)
23 Otter (p. 95)
24 Rock Pipit (p. 94)
25 Oystercatchers (p. 95)

ROCKY SHORE

CLIFFSCAPE

OUT TO SEA

1 Arctic Skua (p. 87)
2 Great Skua (p. 87)
3 Common Porpoise (p. 97)
4 White-beaked Dolphin (p. 97)
5 Knotted Wrack (p. 78)
6 Toothed Wrack (p. 78)
7 Common Winkle (p. 81)
8 Painted Topshell (p. 81)
9 Channelled Wrack (p. 77)
10 Leach's Petrel (p. 95)
11 Bladder Wrack (p. 77)
12 Bottle-nosed Dolphin (p. 97)
13 Storm Petrel (p. 85)
14 Killer Whale (p. 97)

PLANTS

White Rock-rose
Helianthemum apenninum 25 cm
This species is very similar to the Common Rock-rose *H. nummularium*, but it is larger and its leaves are downy grey on both sides as opposed to the latter species which is hairy on only one side. They also have inrolled margins. This low, open, often prostrate, shrubby perennial supports 5-petalled flowers which are bright yellow. It has narrow lanceolate leaves and is very rare in Britain being confined to two sites, Berry Head and Torbay in South Devon. It flowers between May and July.

Sea Campion
Silene vulgaris ssp. *maritima* 15 cm
This species is a common and often abundant plant of sea-cliff ledges, rocky ground and even shingle beaches, and is distributed all around the coasts of the British Isles. It is much shorter than its close relative the Bladder Campion *S. vulgaris* and has smaller, thicker and waxier leaves, which are a shiny greyish-green in colour. Its flowers are larger than the Bladder Campion, are white with 5 very deeply clefted petals. It has a greatly inflated calyx, which is swollen into a purplish or yellowish net-veined bladder. The flowers appear from June to August and they can occur in blankets across the cliff-top.

Rock Sea Spurrey
Spergularia rupicola 20 cm
This perennial grows in short turf, on the broken ground of cliff scree and on walls near the sea. Its completely pink flowers have petals the same size as the sepals and can be found from June to September, followed by the seeds which are all dark brown and unwinged. This species is a stocky perennial, stickily hairy with purplish stems and somewhat silvery stipules. It is a local species in Britain, being found from North Uist south to Cornwall and then eastwards as far as the Isle of Wight. It differs from all other spurrey species in that

the whole plant is densely glandular and hairy.

Hottentot-fig *Carpobrotus edulis* 35 cm
This succulent perennial is a native of South Africa that has become naturalised on the coastal cliffs of Devon, Cornwall, the Isles of Scilly and the Channel Islands. It can reproduce from very small fragments of its roots and will rapidly spread to form complete mats of tangled stems that spread over the whole cliff. The leaves are thick and fleshy and may be as much as 10 centimetres long, reddening at the tip during autumn. The flowers, which appear between May and July, are pink or yellow, with a yellow centre, many petalled and can be up to 10 centimetres across. Although this species can provide a conspicuous show during summer it is easily damaged by frost and thus its range is restricted.

Sea Beet
Beta vulgaris ssp. *maritima* 30–60 cm
This species can be found all around the coast of the British Isles, as far north as the Firth of Forth, and is a characteristic plant of the drift line on shingle beaches. It is, however, found on cliff-tops and can behave as an annual, biennial or perennial. It flowers from July to September, and is very attractive. Its leaves are dark green, hairless, shiny and leathery, triangular nearer the root and wavy nearer the flowers. The tiny, green flowers are held in long, narrow, leafy spikes. Sea Beet often seeds to produce several fruits which often coalesce into a prickly mass. Beetroot and sugar-beet are cultivated forms of this plant.

Common Restharrow
Ononis repens 30 cm
This downy, woody perennial can grow up to 80 centimetres in height and has tough, hairy stems which often creep and sprout roots of their own. Occasionally, and especially when it is found by the sea, the species has a few weak spines. Its leaves

A bed of Sea Pink

grasslands on heaths, roadside verges, meadows and pasture, but it also occurs commonly in the turf above cliff-tops and rocky shores.

Roseroot *Rhodiola rosea* 15–30 cm
This species is a common plant of sea-cliffs in western Scotland and Ireland and may also be found inland where it can grow up to an altitude of 1,200 metres. Its name is derived from the smell of the plant which resembles that of a rose. It is a tufted, greyish succulent, which has short, broad, stiff-toothed and overlapping leaves all up the stem. These are sometimes tinged purplish. The numerous flowers appear in May and June and are held in broad, dense heads and are greenish yellow or sometimes purple tinged in colour. The fruits are orange and the sexes occur on different plants.

are small, well toothed and oval with prominent, toothed, leaf-like stipules half clasping them at their base. It has pink flowers which are superficially broom- or gorse-like. It is widespread and common on dry grassland limestone and dunes, as well as the upper reaches of rocky shores. It flowers from June to September and is well distributed throughout the British Isles, as far north as the Clyde/Moray Firth.

English Stonecrop *Sedum anglicum* 4 cm
This species is perhaps more typical of shingle beaches, but can also be found on the tops of cliffs or amongst rocky scree. It is the commonest of the white stonecrops and it is often initially grey in colour, before turning pink. It has stubby, small and alternate leaves and white star-like flowers which are often tinged pink. These have very short stalks, are held in a short cluster and appear from June until August. The species is widespread in the south west, Wales and the north west of England, the whole of western Scotland and most of western Ireland.

Common Birdsfoot Trefoil
Lotus corniculatus 35 cm
This is one of the commonest and prettiest British members of the pea family. It is an almost hairless perennial which has unstalked trifoliate leaves, each having a lower pair of small oval leaflets which appear like stipules. The flowers, of which 8 may occur in a head, are supported on a longish stalk which is often veined with a reddish or orange tinge. These appear from May onwards, and later give rise to seed pods about 2 centimetres long in a head that resembles a bird's foot and gives the species its name. It is widespread throughout the whole of the British Isles and frequently found inland on short chalk

Biting Stonecrop *Sedum acre* 5–10 cm
This is the commonest of the yellow stone-crops, and can often be found in large mats of tiny, fat, yellow-green leaves which are broadest at their base. It has a peppery taste, conspicuous bright yellow star-like flowers with broad-based petals and is a plant which can be frequently found among maritime rocks and shingle beaches. It is widely distributed over the British Isles, only being absent from parts of north west Scotland and its isles.

Rock Samphire
Crithmum maritimum 30 cm

This species, formerly collected and used for pickling, is easily distinguished by its yellow flowers and succulent blue-green leaves and stems. The flowers are umbelliferous and the leaves cut into narrow, untoothed leaflets and this hairless perennial has a squat bushy appearance with solid stems up to 30 centimetres high. Its fruits are egg-shaped, ridged and corky, and it is found around the south and west coast as far north as Suffolk in the east and Wigtownshire in the west.

Scots Lovage
Ligusticum scoticum 90 cm

This perennial species has distinctive, glabrous, bright green, ternate leaves which were formerly eaten as a vegetable for protection against scurvy. It has stiff-ribbed, usually purplish stems which support the leathery and glossy leaves. The white flowers appear in June and July and the fruits are oval and flattened. This species also often smells of celery or parsley when crushed and large clumps are found on rocky sea cliffs, all around the coasts of Scotland and Northern Ireland.

Shore Dock *Rumex rupestris* 70 cm

This rare perennial flowers in June and July and has characteristic leaves of a blue-green colour. The inflorescence is interrupted and the branching acute, only the lowest whorls having a leaf. The perianths are untoothed with three prominent tubercles. It is very rare in Britain and confined to only 12 locations in Scilly, Cornwall, Devon, Glamorgan, Guernsey, Jersey and Herm in the Channel Islands. It is superficially similar to the Clustered Dock *R. conglomeratus*, but it can be distinguished from this species by its much denser flower spikes, and by its hardy, wavy leaves.

Rock Sea-lavender
Limonium binervosum 12 cm

This perennial grows on dry maritime cliffs, rocks and shingle, and flowers from July to September. It is more slender than Common Sea-lavender *L. vulgare* and has much neater and narrower leaves, each having 1 to 3 unbranched veins and winged stalks. Its flower heads are smaller and the lower branches often flowerless. The leaves are held in a rosette and are broad and lanceolate and the flowers are held on tall round stems. These flowers are a delicate shade of pinky-mauve, and the flat-topped heads are very crowded.

Thrift *Armeria maritima* 5–25 cm

This species is a characteristic and abundant plant of maritime rock and cliff although it can also be common on salt marshes, where it is tolerant of grazing. It also occurs inland as an alpine, especially in the west where it grows on mountain rocks and cliffs to an altitude of 1,300 metres. A tufted perennial it flowers from April to October, but the main period is in June and July when the cushion of single-veined, linear leaves gives rise to many flowers held on leafless downy stalks in compact roundish heads. These occur in a number of shades of pink and in places form a dense carpet over the cliff-top. It is a renowned species and was in the past emblazoned on the reverse of the 3d piece.

Golden Samphire
Inula crithmoides 30–45 cm

This species is a characteristic plant of sea-cliffs and maritime rocks, although it occasionally appears on shingle beaches. A perennial, it flowers in July and August and is our only yellow-rayed daisy-like flower with fleshy leaves. These leaves are linear; run up the entire stem of the plant, and are sometimes 3-toothed at the tip. They are glabrous and succulent in nature and the flowers occur in irregular umbel-shaped clusters, about 2 centimetres across with white, pappus-type fruit. This species is very local on the coasts of Britain, where it is most common in Wales, but it also occurs on a few salt marshes in Essex, Kent and Hampshire.

Goldilocks *Aster linosyris* 50 cm
This woody perennial is very rare and confined to only 7 localities of coastal limestone cliffs in South Devon, Somerset, Glamorgan, Pembrokeshire, Caernarvonshire and South Lancashire. Many of the colonies are small and inaccessible and in the past the plant has suffered from collecting. The bright golden-yellow flowerheads appear in August and September and the unrayed egg-shaped flowers with their yellow stiles and stigmas occur in a loose erect terminal umbel. The leaves are numerous, pale green and linear, and differ from the Golden Samphire which has fleshy leaves. The whole plant has a somewhat spindly appearance.

Carline Thistle *Carlina vulgaris* 45 cm
This stiff, spiny biennial has prickly, thistle-like leaves, the lower of which is cottony. Its flowerheads are placed terminally on the stems, usually in groups of 2 to 5, and support the yellow-brown flowers. These have spiny cotton-type bracts, and conspicuous, purple-based, yellow, sepal-like bracts which fold over in the wet weather. These flowers may often survive the winter appearing superficially similar to those in their living form. The species grows on dry, grazed chalky grasslands as well as on many of our cliff-tops, and it flowers between July and October when it is pollinated by bees and hoverflies.

Spring Squill *Scilla verna* 5–20 cm
This species can be found on dry grassland close to the sea on a wide range of soils, and is a small bulbous perennial which flowers in April and May. The star-like blue flowers and bluish bracts are pollinated by insects and supported on leafless stalks sprouting from a base of very narrow, root leaves. Spring Squill often grows alone, in large beds across the top of cliffs and is well distributed all around the west coast of the British Isles from South Devon to Orkney, and around the Irish coast from County Wicklow to County Londonderry.

Wet Bladder Wrack

Sea Spleenwort
Asplenium marinum 10–30 cm
This small fern is widespread and locally frequent in the cracks and crevices of sea cliffs in the north and west of Scotland. It is a small fern with rather leathery, pinnate, shiny bright leaves. These have oblong, bluntly toothed leaflets which are longest in the middle of the leaf and supported on a brown stalk. The spore cases are arranged in linear heaps on the side veins of the leaflets, and appear between June and September.

Channelled Wrack
Pelvetia canaliculata 15 cm
The wracks are typical seaweeds of rocky shores with strap-like fronds which arise from a disc-shaped holdfast. The Channelled Wrack is olive-brown, becoming greeny-black when dry, and has fronds which are inrolled to form a channel along the length of the frond. The frond ends divide into 2 swollen bags, which have a warty, granular surface. When submerged it hangs downwards with the channelled side inwards towards the rock. This species is common and often abundant around our rocky shores generally up to a metre below the high water mark.

Bladder Wrack *Fucus vesiculosus* 1 m
This olive-brown species differs from the Channelled Wrack in that its fronds are

Fronds of Toothed Wrack

nearly or completely flat. Their edges are wavy and in larger specimens often irregularly torn. It has a prominent midrib on both sides of the blade, which often has pairs of air bladders along its length. The tips of its branches have swollen, granular fruiting bodies. Longer plants tend to have more numerous, longer and rather smaller bladders. The species can be found on the middle shore attached to rocks and is very widely distributed and common around British shores.

Toothed Wrack *Fucus serratus* 90 cm
This species can be separated from the other brown wracks by the serrated edges of its fronds, which also have no bladders. It is not regularly branched and its tips are flat and pointed, but in autumn and winter they may have slight thickenings bearing the fruiting bodies. It can be found on the lower and middle shore on all except the extremely exposed rocky coast, and is widely distributed and common all round the British shores. Its fronds are often marked with the small, white tubes of the worm *Spirorbis*.

Knotted Wrack
Ascophyllum nodosum 90 cm
This species can be easily distinguished from the other wracks. It is olive-green in colour which becomes a blackish-green when dry. Its fronds are irregularly

RIGHT **Strandline decay**

78

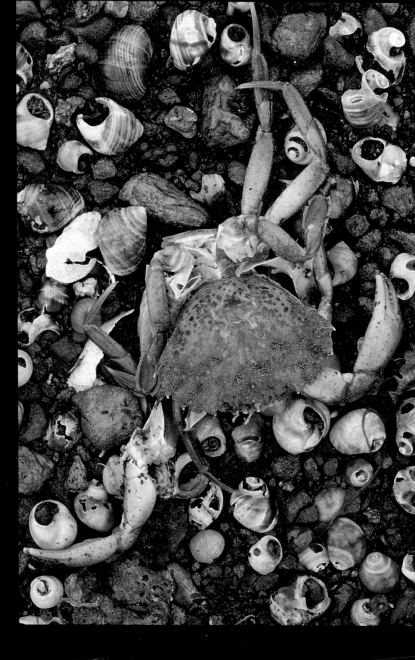

branched, have no midrib and are adorned with single egg-shaped bladders spaced at intervals along the middle of the frond. On sheltered rocky beaches this species may be found in enormous beds which smother the beach. It can be found on the middle shore and is widely distributed and abundant around the British coast.

INVERTEBRATES

Beadlet Anemone *Actinia equina* 4 cm
This species is usually found when the tide is out, when the tentacles are withdrawn into the column to leave a rounded, flat-topped mass of stiff jelly. This is usually a deep browny-red, but cherry red, brownish-green, yellowy-brown or crimson forms also occur. These are occasionally adorned with green spots. When expanded, about 200 tentacles appear in 6 rings which fold in quickly when touched. The top margin of the column is marked with 24 clear blue spots.

The species is widely distributed and common in Britain, on the middle and lower shore on rocks and in pools.

Snakelocks Anemone
Anemonia sulcata 5 cm
This species has about 200 tentacles supported on a rather squat, placid, smooth and even shiny column. These are long, sticky and wavy and unable to contract into the column. The whole animal is usually a dull khaki but can also be pink or a soft apple green with the ends of the tentacles tinged with violet. It can be found in sunny, shallow pools or in rows along the water's edge. In Britain it is distributed all down the west coast, on the western half of the south coast.

Blue-rayed Limpet *Patina pellucida* 2 cm
This species has a small translucent shell, marked with characteristic lines of vivid blue spots from the apex to the margin. The shell becomes more solid as the limpet grows and loses its spots. It can be

Sagartia sphyrodeta

found on the lower shore where it is typically fastened to the stipe or fronds of *Laminaria* seaweeds and it is widely distributed and very common in Britain.

Common Limpet *Patella vulgata* 6 cm
This species has a tall shell with a white or yellowish surface and a head scar which is white or brown in colour. The tentacles which fringe the mantle are projected around the shell when the animal is moving. These are transparent, and the species is conspicuously common on all rocky shores around the British Isles, where it fixes to rocky substrates in groups.

Common or Painted Top Shell
Calliostoma ziziphinum 2 cm
Top shells are broad-based shells which are conical or rounded and often have patches of the underlying mother-of-pearl showing, due to external wear. They always occur on the clean surface of rocks or on weed. The Painted Top Shell is characteristically straight-sided with a flat base, forming a regular pyramid-shaped shell. It is yellow or pink with red streaks, although a white variety also occurs. It is the largest of our top shells and can be found on the lower shore and below, being widely distributed and common around the British coast.

Common Winkle
Littorina littorea 1-2.5 cm
This species has a high and sharply pointed shell with marked sculpturing. The shell is usually dark greyish-black or red and always coloured with darker concentric lines. It is the typical, edible winkle which is regularly harvested for consumption. It is widely distributed on all suitable shores around the British Isles, on the middle shore and below where it attaches to rocks and weed.

Dog Whelk *Nucella lapillus* 2 cm
The whelks are carnivorous species and have thick sculptured shells with a pointed spire and an oval opening. The Dog Whelk can be found on rocks in the barnacle zone, occasionally with mussels, and is usually very numerous. It is off-white, but may also be yellow or banded with brown, and can often be found with egg capsules attached at one end. It likes to seek out crevices, is the chief predator of barnacles and is widely distributed and very common around all of the British shores.

Sea Lemon
Archidoris pseudoargus 5-8 cm
Sea slugs can be the most beautiful animals living on the British shore and are most frequently found during the summer months when they come inshore to spawn and die. All sea slug species only live for one year. They are all carnivorous but have a wide range of feeding habits. The Sea Lemon is the commonest and second largest of the British sea slugs, and feeds on the Breadcrumb Sponge. It lays coiled, white egg ribbons which are about 2 centimetres wide and 5 centimetres long. The animal itself is elliptical in shape with a yellowish foot and an upper surface of yellow, blotched with green, pink or brown. It has 9 tripinnate gills which are retracted very quickly if it is disturbed. It is widely distributed and very common around all of the British shores.

Common Mussel *Mytilus edulis* 10 cm
There are 3 genera of mussels which inhabit the British shores, and these bivalves are frequently harvested for human consumption. The Common Mussel shell is a dark blue, and it can grow up to 10 centimetres in length. It is a very common animal on rocky and stony, but also muddy, shores and even on exposed rocks where it can sometimes be found in dense beds. It is widely distributed and very common on the British coastline.

Common Acorn Barnacle
Balanus balanoides 1.5 cm
There are many species of acorn barnacle, of which this is one of the largest. Its lateral plates overlap one terminal plate, and the

A transparent Common Prawn

width across the area inside the plates is greatest across the middle, giving the whole barnacle a diamond shape. It is a dirty white and can be found on sheltered shores from below the high water to about the low water mark of the spring tides, where it fuses to exposed rocks in conglomerated groups. This species is most common in the north, graduating to common in the south and is only absent from the tip of Cornwall in the British Isles.

Shore Crab *Carcinus maenas* 3–10 cm
This species typically has a dark green shell, the edge of which has 3 blunt teeth between the eyes and 5 more behind the eyes. The last joint of the back legs is flattened for use as a paddle, but also sharply pointed. The tail of the male is 5-jointed, whilst that of the female is 7-jointed and may be carrying a mass of eggs. Shore Crabs can be found on all types of beaches, even in estuaries, on the middle and lower shores and are widely distributed being the commonest crab in the British Isles.

Fiddler or Velvet Crab
Liocarcinus puber 5–13 cm
This species can be distinguished from the Shore Crab by its reddish-brown carapace, which may grow up to 13 centimetres across. Its legs are marked with clear blue joints and lines. Its shell is covered with a fine pile of hair, hence its alternative name, giving it a muddy colour. Its eyes are red, between which 8 to 10 small projections can be seen, as well as 5 larger teeth on either side, on the front edge of the shell. The last joint of the legs is flattened, but unlike the Shore Crab, it is rounded probably to aid swimming. This species is fierce and when disturbed will sit back on its tail holding its pincers up in a defensive position. It can be found on the lower shore and under stones on the south and west coasts of Britain, especially in kelp beds, where it is occasionally very common.

Common Prawn
Palaemon serratus 2–10 cm
The anatomy of the prawns is complicated, because of their many and varied append-

ages, but this is perhaps the most common species of animal you are likely to find in the rock-pools. It can be identified by its long, partly transparent, grey body which is often marked with purplish dots and lines. Its inner antennae are in 3 parts, of which the longest is as long as the body, and the outer antennae may be up to one and a half times as long as the body. The second pair of the legs is longer than the first pair and has much heavier nippers. This species ranges from common to plentiful in pools at the sea's edge, particularly amongst seaweed during August and September. It occurs on the south and west coasts of the British Isles.

Common Starfish *Asterias rubens* 50 cm
Although this species can grow up to 50 centimetres in diameter those found on the shore normally only measure between 5 and 10 centimetres. It normally has 5 arms but occasionally can be seen with 4 or 6. These limbs are rounded, tapered, rough, and well marked with spines down their centres. It is yellowy-reddish-brown, reddish-yellow or even violet with paler markings and is very common on the lower shores of the British coastline.

Spiny Starfish
Marthasterias glacialis 25–30 cm
This species is a typical 5-armed starfish which can occasionally grow up to 70 centimetres in diameter. The body is soft and covered with knobs and spines, so that it is very rough to the touch. It is pale coloured, often ice greenish, yellowish or reddish and if handled will readily throw off its limbs. It can be found on the lower shore on the south and west coasts, although it will normally be found at younger and smaller stages of its life-cycle.

Common Sea Urchin
Echinus esculentus 8–10 cm
This species can occasionally grow up to 15 cm in diameter and is nearly spherical, being slightly flattened at both poles. It is a typical urchin with a brittle limey skeleton,

or test, covered with spines, each moving with a small tubercle. The shell is a deep red, the tubercles white, and the spines are blunt ended, usually marked with purplish tips. It is particularly common in spring, when it can be found on the lower shores. It can be found on nearly every part of the British coast.

VERTEBRATES

Rock Goby *Gobius paganellus* 10 cm
Gobies are remarkably goggle-eyed fish, have 2 dorsal fins and their pelvic fins fuse to form an oval sucker which hangs just clear of the belly line. The Rock Goby has rather uniformly dull and dark coloration and can be identified by a very pale band on top of the anterior dorsal fin. It also has at least 50 scales along its lateral line and its eyes are set so high in the head that their sockets almost touch. It is widespread around the British coast, yet rare in Scotland, and can be very common in the rock-pools where it occurs.

Lumpsucker
Cyclopterus lumpus 12–20 cm
These fish are thick set and rounded with rows of tubercles on their skin. The anterior dorsal fin has been reduced to a row of short lumps and they have a complicated sucker on their underside which is obvious and extraordinarily effective. The male common Lumpsucker is reddish, particularly on the sides and underneath, whilst the female is dark blue to nearly black. They have 4 rows of large tubercles on each side of the body, the whole texture of which is sticky and rough. The posterior dorsal and anal fins balance each other in shape, both above and below the tail. This species is widely distributed round Britain, being commonest in the north and least common in the south.

Father Lasher
Myoxocephalus scorpius 10–20 cm
These solid little fish have spiny gill covers,

broad, rather flattened heads and are browny-grey above, mottled and banded with darker markings. Beneath, they are a whitey-grey with yellow tints and on their sides their lateral line appears paler than the background. The fins are browny-yellow, sometimes banded or spotted with red, and this aggressive species can be found all the way round the British coastline, where it is commonest in the north.

Butterfish *Pholis gunnellus* 8–15 cm
Although rarely, this species may grow to 30 centimetres in length, and is one of the many species of blenny. These are identified by their long dorsal fins, which may be in two or three distinct but connected parts and run from head to tail. The Butterfish's head is heavy, the eyes large and the body a bronzey-grey colour, marked with 10 to 13 white ringed dark spots which run from the base of the dorsal fin to the back. This fin is slightly spined and may have as many as 75 rays. The body is flattened sideways and tapers gently towards a rounded tail. This species earns its name because it is exceptionally slippery and difficult to grasp. It can be found on all coasts and it is very common.

Fulmar *Fulmarus glacialis* 47 cm
This bird is superficially gull-like in appearance but is altogether more blunt, with a very distinctive flight; it glides and banks on stiff wings very close to the waves or cliff-faces. It is further distinguished from gulls by its thick neck, giving the bird a dumpy body, and lack of black tips to its wings. In profile this stiff-winged petrel lacks the inverted V-shape of gulls' wings. Its eyes often appear dark and are quite noticeable, even when the bird is in flight, due to their grey patches. The beak is large with a pronounced tube crowning its top. The species rarely alights on the water, but when it does it swims buoyantly. It can only rise from the water with some difficulty due to the disproportionate size of the wings. It breeds on suitable cliffs and buildings where it shuffles about making a hoarse

Manx Shearwater

cackling or grunting *Ag-Ag-Ag-arr*. It is now a common and regular breeder around the British coast, and can be seen off most beaches, especially those with headlands. Only the eastern coast from Spurn Head down to Portsmouth is lacking in many colonies, although a few can be found in north Norfolk and Kent.

Manx Shearwater *Puffinus puffinus* 35 cm
Like the Storm Petrel this species will only be seen during daylight well away from land, where it can be distinguished from a bevy of other shearwaters by its sharply contrasting black upper-parts and pure white under-parts. It is gregarious and often seen in scattered groups feeding on small, shoaling fish. In flight, long glides are punctuated by a series of quick flaps, the birds banking steeply to show the contrasting pelage. The stiff, narrow wings are set halfway between the tip of the bill and the tail, giving the bird a cross-shaped appearance. Shearwaters swim and dive well, but may also feed in flight. At their nesting burrows they are strictly nocturnal, and at night over the land they make a weird crowing and crooning sound. Their breeding colonies are scattered around the west coast of Britain from the Shetlands down to the Scilly Isles, and also around the Irish coast, and can be identified during daylight by the characteristic honeycombed land surface where

their burrows are hidden. Manx Shearwaters are most often seen on boat trips around the islands during summer, or on spring or autumn passage, when large numbers flock past sea watching points, such as St Ives in Cornwall.

Storm Petrel *Hydrobates pelagicus* 15 cm
This is the smallest European seabird, and will only be seen in daylight out at sea away from its nesting colonies. Here it will often follow ships with its weak, flitting flight just above the waves, at times dancing on the water surface with its dangling black feet. It has longish, blackish wings, a conspicuous white rump, and a squarish, black tail. The underwings have a white wing-bar and the species can be distinguished from Leach's Petrel *Oceanodroma leucorhoa* by its smaller size and shorter wings. The Leach's also has a prominently forked tail. When on land the Storm Petrel makes a sustained rising and falling purring noise from its nesting burrow and this is terminated with a character-istic hiccup. They nest colonially under rocks and in stone walls, laying a single, rounded, white egg in June. They are found predominantly in the north western isles of Scotland, and at other isolated sites in South Wales, Cornwall and the Isles of Scilly.

Gannet *Sula bassana* 95 cm
This bird is quite unmistakable. It is the largest European seabird and has a dazzling, shiny white pelage, with black wing tips in the adults. When seen from the shore the birds' cigar-shaped bodies, deep flapping flight and gliding on angled wings make them conspicuous. These wings flex noticeably at the tips while in flight, and the pointed tail and large, pointed, dagger-shaped bill are also distinctive. Immatures are dusky coloured and closely speckled with white, and in subsequent years become boldly pied blackish-brown and white. When feeding, birds wheel majestically and plunge headlong after fish and, unlike gulls, completely

A gaggle of Gannets

submerge beneath the surface. This species is strictly maritime and can often be seen far out to sea. It returns to shore in spring, and a single, whitish-blue egg is laid in April or May on a bed of seaweed, grass and rubbish. Over 150,000 pairs nest in the British Isles in 17 gannetries, mainly on the Scottish islands, but also on Grassholm, and at Britain's only mainland site at Bempton Cliffs in Yorkshire.

Cormorant *Phalacrocorax carbo* 95 cm
Shag *P. aristotelis* 75 cm
The Cormorant is a large, blackish bird, which can be distinguished from the smaller Shag during the breeding season by its white chin and cheeks, and white patch on the thighs. A breeding Cormorant has bronze wings and is steel blue below, whilst a Shag is greeny-black, instead of bronze, and during the breeding season has a short, upstanding crest. Immature

Shags are distinguished from young Cormorants by their dark brown plumage, lacking any white on the breast.

Both species characteristically extend their wings to dry, but the Shag stretches its wings out further and in flight has more rapid wing-beats. More often seen singly when on the water surface the Shag looks smaller and dives with a noticeable jump under the surface. Recently Cormorants have become more common inland where they can be seen soaring on their large and long wings often to great heights. Both species are colonial nesters laying a single clutch of 3–5 white eggs in April on a nest of rotting vegetation. Both show a westerly distribution around Britain's coasts, Shags being more apparent in the north west and north east of Scotland.

Eider *Somateria mollissima* 60 cm
Although many species of duck may be

Eider down

seen from the rocky shores, including Scaup *Aythya marila*, scoters *Melanitta* spp., mergansers *Mergus* spp. and a host of others, it is this species which is most likely to be found breeding in summer. It can be distinguished from all other ducks by its large size, long heavy body and distinctive flight. This flight is slow and take-off from the surface laboured, and once airborne the bird has a heavy profile. The male Eider is the only British duck with a black belly and white back. It has a pinkish-tinged breast, white forewings, a white head with black crown and pale green patches on its nape, making the bird startlingly conspicuous at sea. The female is brown, closely barred with black and can be distinguished in good visibility from female scoters by their warmer brown and barred plumage.

Gregarious birds, Eiders often fly low, in single file, the females displaying two wing-bars. The male has a low moaning *Coo-roo-uh*, and the species is strongly maritime, often breeding on rocky coasts. In Britain it only occurs north of the Lake District on the west coast, and down as far as Newcastle on the east coast, and it is most commonly found on the north western and north eastern island groups. During winter, however, it can be seen all around the British shores.

Peregrine *Falco peregrinus* 38–50 cm
This crow-sized falcon is distinguished by its long, pointed wings and slightly tapered, short tail. In flight it is pigeon-like, but has shallower wing-beats and long periods of gliding. When perched it can be distinguished by its black moustaches and slate grey upper-parts, which contrast with buffish white under-parts narrowly barred with black. Females are larger than males and often darker, whilst juveniles are dark brown above with streaked not barred under-parts. It is the largest resident falcon in the British Isles, has a distinctive angular shape, and may be detected by the behaviour of many other birds which take to the wing in a general frenzy when it appears.

The Peregrine often soars, but never hovers, and it nests in inaccessible places favouring sea cliffs. Its voice has a wide range, but a repeated *We-chew* and a loud *Kek-kek-kek* are familiarly heard as this arrow-shaped bird winnows menacingly along the cliff-side.

The species is only recently recovering from the ill effects of pesticides and still shows a western bias in the British Isles, being most common in parts of Scotland and Wales, although it is now spreading along the south western coast.

Arctic Skua
Stercorarius parasiticus 46 cm
Great Skua *S. skua* 60 cm
The plumage of the Great Skua is uniformly dark brown, rustier below, and it can be distinguished in flight from all other skuas and immature gulls by its very heavy build, short tail, stout hooked beak and very conspicuous white patch across the base of its primaries. It has broad and rounded wings, which are not pointed like those of the Arctic Skua, and in flight it can be dashing and hawk-like. It settles frequently on water, perhaps more so than the Arctic Skua, which has a very variable pelage ranging from a pale form to an almost all-black form. The Arctic species is the most widespread of the skuas and is a medium-size bird of very distinctive shape. It has a fast flapping flight, interspersed with glides, giving the bird a raptor-like appearance, has projecting central tail feathers and white patches at the base of its primaries. Both species are regular breeders in Britain, but can only be found in the north of Scotland and particularly on the Orkney and Shetland Island groups. They can also be regularly seen on passage all around our coast in spring and autumn.

Kittiwake *Rissa tridactyla* 40 cm
This species is smaller than the Common Gull which is unlikely to be seen on the coast, because it is more frequently found nesting on inland lochs and marshes. The

The last rays of sunlight

Kittiwake has short, blackish legs and a very upright posture when perched, and can frequently be seen following fishing boats. In summer the adult has a pure white head, a greenish-yellow bill and its flight is fairly fast with shallow wing-beats on long, straight, narrow wings. This species is the most marine of the gulls and outside the breeding season spends its time out over the open sea. It has a slimmer wing-shape and distinctive wing markings, which separate it from the Common Gull and a characteristic *Kitiwaka* call which gives the species its name.

It is a colonial, cliff-nesting species, and juveniles have a distinctive W pattern of black banding on their upper wings. They can be separated from Little Gulls *Larus minutus* by their black neckband. The species breeds all around British shores but is most common in the Orkney and Shetland groups.

Lesser Black-backed Gull
Larus fuscus 53 cm
Herring Gull *Larus argentatus* 56 cm
The Herring Gull is the commonest of our

coastal gulls and is readily distinguished from an adult Lesser Black-backed Gull by its paler grey upper-parts. The juvenile is a uniform brown with darker primaries and tail and blackish bill with a paler base, otherwise it may be indistinguishable from the young of the Lesser Black-backed. The latter species is smaller than the Greater Black-backed from which, apart from size, it is often difficult to tell apart. During summer however, the Lesser Black-backed has yellow legs whilst Great Black-backed Gulls have flesh-coloured or pallid legs. The upper parts are a dark slate grey, and both Herring and Lesser Black-backed Gulls produce a repeated strident *Kyow* call when breeding, and also a varied array of barking notes. Both species have a slow, powerful flight, and can be told from the Common Gull and Kittiwake by their larger size. At rest the wings project beyond the tail in the Lesser Black-backed, and this species also has a more delicate head and longer thinner wings. Both species are cliff-top nesters and can

RIGHT **King of the castle**

kyow

be found breeding around most of Britain's shores, the Herring Gull being conspicuously more abundant than the Lesser Black-backed, which shows a north western bias.

Great Black-backed Gull
Larus marinus 70 cm
This bird is much larger than the Herring Gull and Lesser Black-backed Gull, and can be recognised in the summer by its pink legs and its deep *Owk* call note. The largest of all the gulls, its broad wings, jutting head and large bill give the Greater Black-backed Gull a distinctly aggressive appearance. At a distance, without a Lesser Black-backed for comparison, distinguishing it from the latter can be difficult, although the overall colour of the back is much nearer black than the slate grey of the Lesser Black-backed. In flight the birds look slow and unwieldy, but this species is a fierce predator and frequently pursues

weakling or young birds around its cliff-top colonies. During winter it is frequently seen inland, but during the summer it breeds around the western coast of the British Isles, particularly throughout the north western isles of Scotland and the Orkney and Shetland groups.

Guillemot *Uria aalge* 42 cm
Razorbill *Alca torda* 40 cm
Black Guillemot *Cepphus grylle* 34 cm
The Guillemot is distinguished from the Razorbill by its larger size, thinner neck and slender, pointed bill. They are also more brownish than the blacker-coloured Razorbill, and in winter are a grey-brown with white sides of the head and throat and have a conspicuous black line from their eye across their ear coverts. Flight is fast and low, with rapid whirring wing-beats. The head and neck look thinner and longer

RIGHT **Guillemots**

Puffin

whilst the tail is shorter than the Razorbills. In summer, Black Guillemots are distinguished from their larger cousins by their all-black plumage with large white wing patches and bright red feet. During winter their under-parts are white, and their black upper-parts mottled with white. They behave like Guillemots although they are usually seen in smaller numbers, and produce a weak whistling cry, as opposed to the Guillemot's harsh *Arrrrr.*

The Razorbill is black above and white below, and looks more squat than the Guillemot when swimming, carrying its pointed tail cocked upwards. This species is very sociable and perches upright or horizontally on ledges with Guillemots, from which it is easily distinguished at close range by its rather heavy head, shorter thicker neck, and laterally compressed bill. This is distinctly marked midway down with a conspicuous white line which appears to run from the top of the bill to the front of the eye.

Both the Razorbill and Guillemot breed in dense colonies on ledges and steep

LEFT **Razorbill**

cliff-faces, and spend most of their time in coastal and offshore waters. The Black Guillemot however, nests singularly, or in scattered groups, in holes under boulders or on rocky shores, and this species is less common than the former pair. All three species show a westerly bias in the British Isles during the breeding season. The Black Guillemot particularly so, while small numbers of Guillemots and Razorbills can be found on the south western coast and the north eastern coasts of England.

Puffin *Fratercula arctica* 30 cm
This auk's small size, distinctive bill-shape and colour, and dumpy black and white body distinguish it from its cousins the Guillemot and Razorbill. In summer, it has a bright triangular, red, blue and yellow laterally flattened bill and bright orange feet. In winter this bill is somewhat smaller, but still recognisably Puffin-shape. Juveniles have a much smaller bill, but show the typical black and white Puffin face pattern. Puffins are distinctively big-headed, perch upright, but often roost horizontally. Their flight is strong, fast and low over the

waves, with rapid, whirring wing-beats. Puffins sit high in the water, dive well and come ashore to breed in cliff-top burrows during the summer. Most common in the Orkney and Shetland Island groups, smaller numbers of Puffins can be found down the western and north eastern coasts of England, although many of the smaller colonies are now declining.

Rock Dove *Columba livia* 33 cm

This species is the ancestor of the now familiar Feral Pigeon, and as such regularly interbreeds with this type. Consequently true Rock Doves are now judged to only exist in the north western isles of Scotland around the west coast and into the Orkney and Shetland groups, and also along the western and southern coasts of Ireland. Elsewhere copious interbreeding with feral stock has diluted the species. True Rock Doves can be distinguished from Stock Doves and the considerably larger Woodpigeon by their conspicuous white rump and double, broad, black wing bands across their secondaries on the upper wing. Below, their wings are whitish and the tail has a black terminal band, usually with some white on the outer feathers. The rest of the coloration is blue-grey, paler on the back with a glossy green and lilac sheen on the sides of the neck. Although gregarious, they only assemble in small numbers around rocky sea cliffs, where they breed in holes and crevices and are frequently predated by Peregrine falcons.

Rock and Water Pipit
Anthus spinoletta 16 cm

These sub-species are slightly larger and longer than Meadow and Tree Pipits, with longer, much darker legs. The mountain race or Water Pipit *A. s. spinoletta* has white, outer-tail feathers and is the only pipit in summer with unmarked under-parts, which are flushed pinkish during the breeding season. The Rock Pipit has closely streaked, olive-buff under-parts and greyish, not white, outer-tail feathers.

The Rock Pipit generally has a smoky-coloured plumage which makes it easy to distinguish from the rest of the pipits as it perches on rocky scree or beaches. It has a deliberate gait, undulating flight, and makes a distinct *Tsip* call, which sounds more like a Tree Pipit than a Meadow Pipit. In the British Isles this species can be found around most of the coasts, ranging from the Isle of Wight, all around the western coast and down as far as Spurn Head on the eastern coast of England. Only the shores of the eastern and south eastern counties lack this species, but it visits these in winter when it leaves its rocky areas to frequent mud flats and most sea shores.

Chough *Pyrrhocorax pyrrhocorax* 40 cm

These birds are most often seen wheeling overhead in large flocks, calling distinctively, and performing insane aerobatics. The call is a distinct high pitched *Kee-ow* and the flight is strong, buoyant, the wings having separated and upcurved primaries when soaring. It can be distinguished from a Jackdaw by the absence of any grey plumage, and at rest by its longer, conspicuously red bill and bright red legs. It inhabits cliffs, quarries and ruins but nowadays is most easily seen on parts of the Welsh coast and the Isle of Man. Small numbers also breed on the south western isles of Scotland, but the species' stronghold in the British Isles is the western Irish coast.

Raven *Corvus corax* 65 cm

The easy soaring flight and regular, powerful wing-beats identify this species which, for all its bulk, is incredibly acrobatic, especially during courtship. At rest its massive, black bill, shaggy throat feathers and wedge-shaped end of tail make it distinctive from all of the smaller crows. Its plumage is black and iridescent in sunlight and its voice is a deep, often repeated *Prruk-prruk*. Ravens are usually seen in pairs and frequent inland rugged terrain as well as coastal cliffs. Despite a decline in numbers they are commonest on the west coast of the British Isles, ranging from Cornwall, through Wales and into western and northern Scotland, and its associated islands.

Many other species of birds will regularly be seen on visits to rocky shores and cliff habitats. Carrion Crows *Corvus corone* are often picking through mussel beds with groups of Oystercatchers *Haematopus ostralegus* and these noisy, conspicuous waders are often joined by Turnstones *Arenaria interpres*, Ringed Plover *Charadrius hiaticula* and in winter by Purple Sandpipers *Calidris maritima*, small, yellow-legged and very darkly coloured birds which show a conspicuous white wing-bar in flight. Buzzards *Buteo buteo*, Golden Eagles *Aquila chrysaetos* and Kestrels *Falco tinnunculus* are all regular sea-cliff-nesting raptors, the former pair showing a north western bias in the British Isles. In winter large numbers of Common Scoter *Melanitta nigra*, Velvet Scoter *M. fusca*, Long-tailed Duck *Clangula hyemalis*, Goldeneye *Bucephala clangula* and Scaup *Aythya marila* can be seen offshore from many rocky promontories.

In spring and autumn Little Shearwaters *Puffinus assimillis*, Great Shearwaters *P. gravis*, Sooty Shearwaters *P. griseus*, Cory's Shearwaters *Calonectris diomedea* and Leach's Petrel *Oceanodroma leucorhoa* can all be glimpsed on passage as they wend their way to or from their breeding grounds. At such times these coastal cliff-tops act as dropping sites for many passage visitors and rarities. These join Meadow Pipits *Anthus pratensis*, Skylarks *Alauda arvensis*, Wheatears *Oenantle oenanthe* and Stonechats *Saxicola torquata* on the grassy tops of the shores or cliffs and add to the diversity of this bird-dominated environment.

Otter *Lutra lutra* 96–140 cm
These days this species is most easily seen in the secluded parts of the north west and north of Scotland and their associated isles. In water it can be distinguished from Mink and other aquatic rodents by its larger, flattened head, long tapering tail, and large V-shaped wake. Its swimming movements are not jerky, but are smooth. Its pelage appears glossy when wet and spiky after it has shaken. It is a uniform brown except for a paler throat and on land it moves with a typical mustelid bounding gait. The droppings or spraints are deposited at regular sites often on top of a rock, mound of soil, or mat of grass, and can be identified by their contents such as fish scales and bones and mollusc shells.

Common Seal *Phoca vitulina* 120–160 cm
Grey Seal *Halichoerus grypus* 165–230 cm
These species are not easily separated by the colour of their pelage, which is basically a mottle of dark spots on a lighter ground colour, usually darker above and lighter below. However, the Common Seal has a much more pleasing expression, with a rounded head and a separate dog-like nose, whilst the Grey Seal has a forehead which slopes into a rather unappealing Roman nose. Only in the young is the head-shape of the Grey Seal similar to the Common Seal. Another distinguishing feature is the nostrils; those of the Common Seal form a V-shape whilst those of the Grey Seal are parallel and separate. On soft substrates both species leave clear tracks and when out of the water Common Seals frequently adopt a head-up, tail-up attitude. Common Seals occasionally porpoise at sea, leaping clear of the water and these are more sedentary than the wandering Grey Seal. The latter species is more typical of exposed rocky coasts and caves, and their largest breeding populations occur on offshore islands such as the Farnes and many of the Orkneys, whilst the Common Seal frequents shallow sheltered waters. Thus it is the characteristic seal of sandbanks, mudbanks and estuaries, and its biggest population is found in The Wash of East Anglia. The North Sea population has recently been decimated by a viral infection.

Common Porpoise
Phocoena phocoena 1.8 m

This species is the commonest British cetacean, and is found all around the British coast. It can frequently be seen from cliff-tops and its general short, robust form makes it distinguishable from most of our other cetaceans. It has no beak, a low receding forehead and occurs in small to large schools where it does not normally leap clear of the water as do dolphins. Its back is black and its belly white, with a varying amount of grey on the sides, and it has a black streak from its mouth to its flippers. This species feeds on Herring, Sole and Whiting, and produces a single calf from July onwards.

Killer Whale *Orcinus orca* 4.6–9.2 m

This powerfully built robust cetacean has no beak and is easily distinguished by its back fin, which may be up to 1.8 metres high in adult males. Predominantly black above they have a grey saddle behind this dorsal fin, and are very fast swimmers. They may be gregarious, often gathering in large packs when hunting for whales, dolphins, porpoises, seals, and large fish. They have a worldwide distribution but are fairly common in British waters and are best seen from the north western isles and the Hebrides in Scotland.

White-beaked Dolphin
Lagenorhynchus albirostris 3.5 m

This species is usually seen in large schools and is predominantly a northern species in British waters, more often seen in the North Sea than on the west or south coasts. It frequently becomes stranded when its short but conspicuous white snout and fairly large dorsal fin can be seen, while in the water it often leaps clear of the surface revealing white sides and belly. It feeds on Herring, Cod and Whiting, and undergoes an annual migration between temperate and sub-polar waters.

LEFT **Oystercatchers**

Bottle-nosed Dolphin
Tursiops truncatus 3.7 m

Generally slower than the smaller dolphins, this species congregates into small schools during the breeding season and is migratory in the North Atlantic. It can be seen in British waters during the summer, where it feeds on a wide variety of fish and cuttlefish. It is the most frequently seen species after the Common Porpoise, and is often found in the south and west of the English Channel. It has a receding low forehead, a prominent back fin and is slate grey or light brown in colour, having a pale pink throat and dark-coloured flippers.

With the exception of Rabbits *Oryctolagus cuniculus* and domestic animals, primarily sheep *Ovis* spp. and goats *Capra* spp. and their various feral forms, there are no grazing animals associated with rocky shores. No doubt a few Foxes *Vulpes vulpes* prey on these and the occasional Field Vole *Microtus agrestis*, and their island subspecies, which try to eke out a meagre existence in the harsh environment of the shore line and cliff-top. Bats *Chiroptera* are probably much under-recorded, and may use cliff crevices as roost-sites more often than is assumed. The Greater Horseshoe Bat *Rhinolophus ferrumequinum* certainly uses some seaside cliff caves as roost-sites. Cetaceans can be regularly seen from our shores in certain places but they are less readily identified by the novice since half of them or more is generally beneath the surface and there are many candidates in the whale, porpoise and dolphin family Cetacea, that can be seen from the British coastline.

Of the seals, family Pinnipedia, the Ringed Seal *Phoca hispida* can occasionally be seen in Scotland, the Harp Seal *P. groenlandicus* was formally recorded here, before its persecution in North America, as was the Bearded Seal *P. barbetus*. The Hooded Seal *Cystophora cristata* and Walrus *Odobenus rosmarus* have also been seen from British shores, even in recent years.

BRITISH ROCKY SHORE NATURE RESERVES

What follows is a list of nature reserves, managed by various bodies, which the public can visit (but sometimes only after special application for a permit) to see many of the species mentioned in this book. These reserves show a bias towards cliff sites, and seabird colonies in particular, and access to the shore line itself here may often be difficult, dangerous or impossible. Attempting to list the location of all rocky shores around the thousands of miles of the British coastline would be impossible, so I would suggest that if you wish to explore rock-pools in the absence of thousands of wheeling, screaming birds you enquire more locally as to the nearest source of these to your home. A telephone call to your local Naturalist Trust may be all that is required.

ENGLAND

Avon

The coastline of Avon lacks any real rocky cliff reserves, although some land slipping may be found on the **North Hill Nature Trail** (SS 968474) and the **Somerset and North Devon Coast Path** (SS 793487–971467). The nearest sea cliff reserves and rocky shores are in North Devon and Cornwall, easily accessible from the M5.

Bedfordshire and Huntingdonshire

Almost centrally placed in England, these counties are obviously lacking in any rocky seaside or cliff habitat. Their eastern bias also separates them from the Welsh coastline, so to visit any cliff in this area means a considerable journey into the

LEFT **Silvery silhouette**
RIGHT **A loitering Gannet**

north of England or Wales, unless the few miles of steep cliffs found at Hunstanton in Norfolk satiate the investigator.

Berkshire

Placed in central southern England, Berkshire too is obviously devoid of any seaside or cliff habitat; however the cliff coastlines of Dorset and Sussex are now easily accessible due to the modern motorways. Alternatively the M4 leads from the east counties all the way into the cliff-land of South Wales. Either way when you visit cliffs from Berkshire it means a day out.

Buckinghamshire

In some parts of this county you are probably further from the sea than anywhere else in England, and consequently a specific journey will be needed to encounter any sea cliff or rocky shore habitat. This would require a trip to South or North Wales or northern England, but the central position of the county means that a journey of similar distance would bring you to the cliffs of Dorset or Sussex on the south coast.

Cambridgeshire

Placed in the east of England the cliff-sides of the south and west, and of Wales may seem too far a journey for some investigators. However, the cliffs at Hunstanton in Norfolk are only an hour away for most of the county, and access to the north east coast of England is also relatively easy using the modern roads, providing they are not being mined and lined with strings of infamous cones.

Cheshire

Although this county has some sea coast around the perimeter of the Wirral it is mostly low lying, if not heavily industrialised. However, the coastline of North Wales is within easy access using the A55 route, and the M6 will lead you quickly into the cliff-side habitat of the north west coast and the Lake District.

Cornwall

The Chapel Porth Nature Trail.
SX 697495 3.2 km.
Cornwall County Council.
Gannets, Guillemots, Kittiwakes and Fulmars are the seabird complement to this range of rocky cliffs, whilst Ravens and Buzzards may also be seen. The trail encompasses a range of habitats including a deep valley, some coastal heathland, and some exceptional rocky cliffs.

Isles of Scilly. 1,600 ha. Duchy of Cornwall – Nature Conservancy Council.
This small group of islands numbers forty or more, and includes some rocky coastline. Annet is an important breeding site for Manx Shearwaters, Storm Petrels, Puffins and many thousands of gulls. Guillemots and Razorbills also nest here with Fulmars and Kittiwakes. Although the island is closed from April to August, to protect the breeding birds, it is worth an out-of-season visit to investigate its botanical and other avian interest.

Kynance Cliffs. SW 688132. 26 ha.
Cornwall Trust for Nature Conservation (C.T.N.C.).
These cliffs have many of the plants found on the Lizard Peninsular such as Cornish Heath, Bog Asphodel, Tawny Sedge, Yellow Centaury and Three-lobed Crowfoot, and also provide nesting-sites for many birds.

The Lizard. SW 701140. 400 ha.
Various bodies.
The complicated geology of this area has given rise to soil formations which support a very special array of plants. The

heathland on top of the cliff has stretches of mixed gorse and heather, and varies from wet to dry heath. Dwarf Rush, Pigmy Rush, Dorset Heath, Chives, Spring Squill and Cornish Heath make a wonderful show, whilst Pillwort, and the very rare *Erica williamsii* can all be found. Part of this area includes the lower **Predannack cliffs** (SW 660163. 16 ha. C.T.N.C.), and this reserve holds a similarly magnificent range of plants above the cliffs themselves. These include dwarf varieties of Betony, Ox-eye Daisy, Common Knapweed and Devil's-bit Scabious, and prostrate varieties of Wild Asparagus, Broom, Dyer's Greenweed, Privet and Juniper. Also found are uncommon species such as Twin-flowered, Upright and Long-headed Clover, Fringed Rupturewort, Spring Sandwort, Thyme Broomrape and Hairy Greenweed, whilst the lower rocky areas are encrusted with lichens and plants such as Navelwort.

South West Peninsular Coast Path.
SS 212174–SX 455534. 427 km.
Countryside Commission.
This path runs from Plymouth in the south to the Marsland valley in the north and encompasses miles of spectacular coastline. The majority of species of birds mentioned in this book can be seen, either in residence or visiting from other offshore sites. The cliffs may be up to 200 metres high and are topped with dwarf shrub heathland or sloping grassland and here Thrift, Common Birdsfoot Trefoil, Ling, Bell Heather and Bristlebent Grass are typical, whilst more unusual plant species include Hairy Greenweed, Shore Dock, Slender Birdsfoot Trefoil and the parasitic Carrot Broomrape. An interesting and unusual species is the *coccinea* variety of Kidney Vetch, which is a dark, dusky red instead of the more typical yellow found over the rest of Great Britain. Other specialities include Golden Samphire, Rock Sea Spurrey, Sea Spleenwort, and a host of other species which enjoy the warm sea air and the array of soils formed from the granite, gabbro, dolomite, basalt and serpentine rocks.

Butterflies to be found include Green Hairstreak, Dark Green, Pearl-bordered and Small Pearl-bordered fritillaries, Dingy and Grizzled Skipper and Marbled Whites.

Cumbria

St Bee's Head. NX 959118. 5 km. Royal Society for the Protection of Birds.
On Cumbria's westernmost point, this reserve has a path which climbs the cliffs amongst a changing pattern of soil. Thrift, Harebell, Sheeps' Bit, Wild Thyme and Restharrow give way to Ling, Bell Heather, Gorse and Meadow Saxifrage; Orpine and Rock Samphires are also present. Birds include Herring Gull, Kittiwake, Fulmar, Guillemot, Black Guillemot and Razorbill. Many thousands of Puffins nest on the sandstone cliffs. Rock Pipit, Kestrel, Raven, Linnet, Stonechat and Whitethroat are also present, whilst Peregrine and Merlin hunt in the reserve, and offshore birds to be found include terns, Gannets and Manx Shearwaters. In winter Common Scoter and Red-throated Diver visit the seas visible from the path.

Derbyshire

As an inland county Derbyshire is not starved of cliff habitat, since the dales include many steep limestone escarpments. However, to investigate sea cliffs and their rocky shores a journey is needed either into North Wales or north west or north eastern England, all of which are easily accessible.

Devon

Berry Head County Park. SX 943564. 43 ha. Torbay Borough Council.
White and Rock Stonecrop, Sea Campion and Thrift can be found on the shallow curves abutting the sheer cliffs. The ice-age relics, White Rock-rose, Hornwort,

Goldilocks and Slender Hare's-ear occur here and in few other places in Britain, and Berry Head holds one of the few south coast colonies of Auks. Guillemot and Razorbill are joined by other seabirds such as Fulmar and Kittiwake, whilst Jackdaws and Rock Doves also use the cliffs as breeding sites. These cliffs, and those found in a nearby quarry also provide roosting sites for several bat species and the park also provides an ideal place for looking out to sea and watching the Cormorants and Gannets passing the reserve.

Lundy. SS 143437. 450 ha.
Landmark Trust–National Trust.
This sea-battered island, about 5 kilometres long and less than 1 kilometre wide, is situated some 20 kilometres off the North Devon coast. Its western cliffs are high and some forty species of birds nest around the island, including Puffin, Guillemot, Razorbill, Fulmar, Kittiwake and Shag, whilst Lesser and Greater Black-backed Gulls and Herring Gulls nest amongst the cushions of Thrift and banks of heather, bracken and grasses. Manx Shearwater still breed, as do Raven, Wheatear and Rock Pipit. Of special interest to botanists is the Lundy Cabbage which grows nowhere else in the world and supports two species of beetle, which are also similarly isolated.

The North West Peninsular Coast Path.
North Devon SS 213174–793487.
South Devon SX 493531–SY 332916.
256 km. Countryside Commission.
Devon has two separate coastlines: the north is entirely hard rock and exposed to the raging Atlantic, and the south has softer rocks and includes the Tamar, Plym, Yelm, Fern and Avon estuaries. Both paths encompass a wide variety of rocky shores and cliffs and support an equally wide range of zoological and botanical interest.

Dorset

Durlston Country Park. SZ 032773.
105 ha. Dorset County Council.
Here Jurassic limestone cliffs stand exposed to the brunt of the elements, and from these steeply sloping areas superb views of seabirds and their nesting colonies can be had. Above these slopes a great variety of lime-loving plants can be found: Common Birdsfoot Trefoil, Kidney and Horseshoe Vetch, Lady's Bedstraw and Salad Burnet join Restharrow, Yellow-Wort and Common Centaury, Carline Thistle, Dwarf Thistle and Quaking Grass. Pyramidal Orchid, Greater Knapweed and Wild Parsnip can also be found as can a range of butterflies which includes Adonis, Chalkhill and Small Blues, Marbled Whites, Dark Green Fritillaries and Lulworth Skippers.

Isle of Portland. SY 682738. 1,050 ha.
Various bodies.
This massive limestone outcrop is famed as a superb site for sea watching, and its bird observatory and ringing station play host to a bevy of migrational rarities. Nesting Herring Gulls, Guillemots and Razorbills join a few Puffins on the cliffs, and a range of typical botanical interest can be found along the few accessible rocky slopes.

Lulworth Range Walks. SY 882804.
Ministry of Defence.
These walks, of various lengths, run over the Ministry firing range, which is still in use. Visitors must keep to the marked footpaths and observe that access is only open on non-firing days. Enquiries to Bindon Abbey 462721 ext. 859. Ten and a half kilometres of paths stretch over this area, much of which is spectacular in a geological perspective. Many of the typical birds, plants and butterflies of the cliff-side and upper slope habitat can be seen and there are many rocky shores to investigate.

Purbeck Marine Reserve. SY 909788. 650 ha. Dorset Naturalist Trust.

An Information Centre can be found at Kimeridge Bay, a deep curve of shaley cliffs which fall into the Kimeridge ledges, and from here over 7 kilometres of cliffs can be explored. Some are up to 165 metres in height, many are unstable, and overall they provide an enormous range of coastal habitat. The difference in height between high and low tide is less than 2 metres but a wide area of rocky shore is exposed at low water, and because the reserve is midway between the western and eastern basins of the English Channel it contains several species on the limits of their normal distribution, including Cushion Starfish, Wartlet Anemone and Pandora Shell.

South West Coast Path.
SY 344928–SZ 042860. 116 km.
Countryside Commission.

This path runs from Lyme Regis to Poole harbour and thus traverses large areas of cliff-type habitat, much of which is spectacular in nature. Botanically it is interesting, but in terms of birds there are none of the large exciting colonies found in the north of the country although Peregrine, Buzzard, Kestrel, Jackdaw, Kittiwake and Herring Gull can all be seen.

Whitenothe Undercliff. SY 765813. 46 ha. National Trust–Dorset Naturalist Trust.

Cliffs up to 140 metres high overlook a great sweep of Weymouth Bay and the Isle of Portland, and landslips have formed a series of slopes, terraces and gullies which are covered with a wide range of plants. Kestrel and Buzzard occur and the warm banks are frequently used as sunning sites for adders. Lulworth Skipper and great green bush-cricket, which is the largest bush-cricket in Northern Europe, provide the insect interest.

Durham, Cleveland and Tyne-and-Wear

Black Hall. Permit only. 32 ha. Durham County Conservation Trust.

This limestone cliff is clay-topped and Blue Moor-grass, Bird's-eye Primrose, Bloody Cranesbill and Large Wintergreen can be found, along with Grass of Parnassus in the damp places. Common Rock-rose, Restharrow, and Common Birds-foot Trefoil join a fine display of orchids and a wide variety of insects, including many Common Blue and some of the isolated Castle Eden Argus butterflies. This particular form of Argus butterfly is only found in this north eastern coastal strip and its caterpillars feed only on Common Rock-rose.

Marsden Cliffs. NZ 397650. 1 km.
South Tyneside N.B.C.

This stretch of limestone cliffs holds the most important colonies of breeding Kittiwakes, Fulmars, Cormorants and Herring Gulls between the Farne Islands (Northumberland) and Bempton Cliffs (Yorkshire). They are joined by a few pairs of Lesser Black-backed Gulls and a range of typical plants, including Common Rockrose and Thrift.

Essex

Whilst this county has a wide range of estuarine and salt marsh habitats it is entirely lacking in any rocky shores. Its eastern position makes most of the dramatic scenery of the north east, north west and south west seem very distant. The closest cliff habitat would be the comparatively inert chalk cliffs in Kent and Sussex.

Gloucestershire

This predominantly low lying county is entirely lacking in any rocks or steep-sided seaside escarpments, but access to South Wales via the M4, A40 or A38 is easy.

Greater London

From this area any visit to a rocky seaside habitat means a day trip. From its central position the closest cliffs would be the chalk of Sussex and Kent; further west those of Dorset; and a little further afield those of North Devon or South Wales.

Hampshire and the Isle of Wight

The mainland of Hampshire, despite its wide range of estuarine and salt marsh habitats, is entirely lacking in sea cliffs or rocky shores. But on the Isle of Wight . . .

Tennyson Down and The Needles.
SU 324855. 78 ha. National Trust.
The northern side of this reserve falls steeply to Alum Bay, the south side has sheer cliffs of chalk and the western end is weathered into the stacks of The Needles. The plateau is 147 metres above sea level, and supports many chalkland plants stunted by seawinds, including pygmy variations of Clustered Bellflowers, short-stemmed Harebells, and the well-adapted Dwarf Thistle. Masses of Kidney Vetch, Thrift, Wild Mignonette and Pyramidal Orchids overlook The Needles, with a few of the normally beach-loving Yellow Horned Poppy. Although the colonies of Guillemot, Razorbill and Puffin are now depleted there are still a variety of gulls, Cormorants, Shags and Jackdaws to be seen along with the occasional Peregrine and range of offshore seabirds.

Herefordshire and Worcestershire

From this central western area the rocky shores and cliffs of South and North Wales are easily accessible and provide the easiest and closest access to this type of habitat.

Huntingdonshire

Being almost centrally placed in England, visiting cliffs from this county requires at least a day out. The closest would be those in Kent and Sussex, but it is a considerable journey to the south west or north east to find something a little more spectacular, including any seabird colonies.

Kent

This area of chalk grassland, landslips and open cliffs has plants including Sea Heath, Rock Sea-lavender and Privet, and is one of the best sites in southern England for migrant butterflies.

North Downs Way.
TQ 428557–TR 319412. 123 km.
Countryside Commission.
Part of this old Pilgrim's way from Winchester to Canterbury runs along the sea coast, over the white cliffs to Dover, and although this primarily downland habitat can be explored, access to the actual cliff-sides is dangerous, restricted, or impossible, as is most of the chalk cliff-land of Kent. Visitors will have to be content with views down the cliff at the many Jackdaws, Kestrels and occasional Peregrines.

Lancashire and Greater Manchester

Despite the Irish sea coast this region has no rocky shores. The frontage is much shallower and, although several fine estuarine salt marsh areas can be explored, one would need to visit either North Wales or Cumbria to find typical cliff habitat.

Leicestershire and Rutland

Placed in central England this area is devoid of any coastline, but well situated to permit daytrips to North Wales or the north Norfolk coast. Any short trips to the north or south of England cliff habitats are probably however precluded by the distances involved.

Lincolnshire and South Humberside

This region has some sea frontage facing the North Sea. It is, however, devoid of any steep terrain and the nearest cliffs would be those further north on the east coast in Yorkshire or the isolated number on the north Norfolk coast.

Norfolk

Hunstanton Cliffs. TF 674417. 1 km.
Public access to beach.
Although this area has a characteristic cliff type of topography the cliff-top is a lawn and the shore is a mass of crumbled chalk, neither of which supports much interesting plant fauna. The cliffs are of Carstone overlain by chalk and do have breeding Fulmars, which colonised in 1964, and in winter the foreshore plays host to Purple Sandpipers.

Northamptonshire

This region's central placing in England precludes any day visits to cliff-side habitats, with the exception of the Hunstanton Cliffs in Norfolk, due to the long distances involved. Special trips would be needed to place the cliffs in the north east of England, Wales or the south of England at the reach of the explorer.

Northumberland

Farne Islands. NU 230370. 32 ha.
National Trust.
This group of 28 small islands, the largest of which is Inner Farne, is a superb place to see and explore the cliff habitat. A boat service runs, during fair weather, from Seahouses on the mainland and for a few pounds the boat master will put you ashore amongst thousands of squabbling sea-birds. These include vast numbers of nesting Terns. From the many paths Guillemots, Razorbills, Puffins, Cormorants, Shags and Fulmars can be easily observed at close range, along with Eider, Kittiwake and Lesser Black-backed Gulls. The relatively low cliffs are topped with typical botanical interest, including carpets of Bluebells, Thrift and Bladder Campion, but this group of islands is also renowned for its colony of Grey Seals. This species breeds here and may be seen from the cliff-tops and during the boat trip.

Nottinghamshire

Lacking any sea coast a specific trip is required to explore rocky shore habitat from this region. The Yorkshire coastline or that of North Wales are both accessible to the explorer, but require more than a day out to fully enjoy each area.

Oxfordshire

This central region is well placed via the M4 to permit visits to the South Wales or North Devon and Cornwall coasts where the nearest cliff habitat can be found. Alternatively the investigator may choose to travel south to Dorset via the M3.

Shropshire and Staffordshire

Situated on the Welsh border this region has easy access to all parts of the Welsh coast which contains a wide range of excellent cliff habitats for the investigator to explore. Most regions are easily accessible for a day trip.

Suffolk

With the exception of some low, sandy cliffs adjacent to Dunwich Common, Suffolk's coastline is devoid of any rockier or steeper topography. It does however have some of Britain's finest wetland reserves, but for the intent cliff-face or rock-pool explorer a considerable journey is needed either to the south, west or north.

Surrey

From this region of southern England the nearest cliff habitat is the chalk of Kent. Access to the cliffs is difficult and their inhabitants not nearly so diverse as those found along more westerly and north westerly shores. Consequently a considerable journey is required in order to explore any true cliff habitat from this region. Access to the west via Dorset may be difficult whilst the completed M25 and M4 may lead the observer more easily to South Wales.

Sussex

Beachy Head Nature Trail. TV 586956. 2 km. Eastbourne Borough Council.
This circular trail ranges over the chalk headland with its range of plants. These include Kidney Vetch, Wayfaring Tree, and several species of orchid, whilst butterflies include 5 species of blues.

Cuckmere Haven. TV 519995. 392 ha. East Sussex County Council–Lewes District Council.
This area, where rolling chalk hillsides have been sliced to form stark white cliffs, is subdivided into the Seven Sisters Country Park and Seaford Head. Only three of the famous Seven Sisters lie within the country park, but several unusual plants grow on them. Field Fleawort, Burnt Orchid and Round Headed Campion join Common Sea-Lavender and Sea Radish. Moon Carrot, Least Lettuce and Small

Hare's-ear are also rather isolated species and many other more typically downland species, including several orchids and gentians, can be found on the grassland above the cliffs. These are the highest chalk cliffs in Britain and hold nesting Jackdaw, Herring Gull and Fulmar, whilst they are occasionally visited by Peregrines. The cliff-top grassland is home for many species of warbler, Stonechat, and a host of passage birds and the whole reserve encompasses a wide range of habitats, other than the cliffside. It is a superb place to explore any of these, perhaps directed from the Information Centre which publishes a trail guide and has a reference library.

Hastings Country Park Nature Trails.
TQ 860118. Hastings Borough Council.
These sandstone sea cliffs hold nesting seabirds and are topped by gorse and heather heathland and may be worth a visit during spring or early summer.

Warwickshire and the West Midlands

Centrally placed in the British Isles this region is obviously devoid of coastline. However, the Welsh cliffs, both in the north and the south are easily accessible, as are those in north Devon via the M5.

Wiltshire

The rocky shores of Dorset are easily accessible from this region, and if the explorer seeks a little more diversity those of North Devon and South Wales are similarly accessible.

Yorkshire and North Humberside

Bempton Cliffs. TA 197738. 4.8 km. Royal Society for the Protection of Birds.
For many people living in central or eastern England these cliffs will be the most

106

accessible, and as such are well worthy of a visit. They hold Britain's only mainland gannetry and have 33 regularly breeding bird species, including thousands of auks (Guillemot, Razorbill and Puffin), Jackdaws, Rock Pipits, Rock Doves and the occasional Peregrine. Whilst there may be over 350 pairs of Gannet there are more than 65,000 pairs of Kittiwake and all the splendour of a seabird colony can be experienced peering over the edge of these 120 metre high chalk cliffs. During summer the cliff-tops have 15 butterfly species and several rare insects, including the Great Yellow Bee. During the autumn and winter they also provide a good vantage point for sea watching.

Filey, North Cliff. TA 115813. 46 ha. Scarborough Borough Council.

A nature trail and bird hide have been provided for visitors to explore the cliffs and coastline of Filey Brig.

WALES

Clwyd

Despite this region's lack of rocky or steeper seaside topography it has several interesting areas of salt marsh and estuary. However, it is within easy reach of the rocky shores and cliff habitats of Gwynedd.

Dyfed

Bosherston Ponds and Stackpole Head. SR 966948. 797 ha. National Trust.
The cliffs fronting this sea-drowned valley are very variable. They range from a series of shelves to a sheer drop to the sea's edge and natural arches, stacks and blow holes can be explored. Plants include Rock Sealavender, Thrift, Rock Sea Spurrey and Golden Samphire, whilst the cliffs provide nesting sites for a colony of seabirds.

Cardigan Island. Permit only. 16 ha. West Wales Naturalists' Trust.
This small island has 900 breeding pairs of Herring Gull, along with Greater and Lesser Black-backed Gull, Fulmar, Shag, Oystercatcher, Jackdaw and Rock Pipit. Non-breeding Kittiwake often occur, and other visitors include Chough and Raven.

Elegug Stacks. SR 926945. 1 ha. Ministry of Defence – Pembrokeshire Coast National Park Authority.
These coastal cliffs are well worth a visit. Parking is only a few metres away from spectacular breeding sites for Guillemot and Razorbill. Kittiwakes can be observed at very close range by peering into blow holes, and a typical range of cliff-top plants can be seen.

Pembrokeshire Coast National Park.
58,275 ha. Pembrokeshire Coast National Parks Authority.
A coast path (SN 164468–174073. 270 km) runs the length of the park and stretches from Cardigan to Amroth, and includes some of the most interesting and accessible rocky shored habitat in the British Isles. The geology is diverse and interesting, as is the wildlife which thrives here. The park includes the Scomer Island Complex, St David's Head and Bosherton Ponds, and a walk along the coast path will bring the explorer within easy access of many of the species referred to in this book.

Penderi Hanging Oakwood. SN 550732. 12 ha. West Wales Naturalists' Trust.
Whilst Cormorant, Shag and Herring Gull nest on the cliffs over the sea, and Grey Seals gather in autumn and occasionally breed in the more sheltered bays, it is the oakwoods above the sea cliff which make this area more interesting. These have been severely stunted by exposure to gales, yet still hold a variety of woodland plants and birds.

Ramsey Island. SM 700235. 200 ha.
This island holds the most important breeding colony of Grey Seals in Wales, and its cliffs support the best population of the now rare and beautiful Chough. It has a range of geology and supports an unusual range of plants and generally is exceptionally worthy of a visit. Boat trips to this Island run from St Justinians from June to September (Telephone 0437 720648).

St David's Head. SM 734272. 208 ha.
National Trust.
This is a popular beauty spot, but away from the car parks it is also a fine area for the naturalist to explore. The grassland which runs to the cliff-edge is typical and includes Ling, Bell Heather, gorse and Tormentil, and steep gorse and bracken covered slopes run in a great arc to Strumble Head, where the headland slants to form steep gullies dropping towards the sea. Sea Spurrey, Biting Stonecrop and English Stonecrop join Orpine, Sea-lavender, Chives, Hairy Greenweed, and the dwarf coastal form of Ox-eye Daisy. The cliffs provide nesting-sites for Buzzard, Raven, small numbers of Chough and many seabirds.

St Margaret's Island. Permit only. 5.6 ha.
West Wales Naturalists' Trust.
Landing on this small island can often be dangerous and is by permit only. In summer, boat trips run around the island to see the huge colonies of Cormorant, Kittiwake, Razorbill, Guillemot and Great Black-backed Gull. Manx Shearwater can be seen regularly and the pretty Storm Petrel occasionally, as well as most of our other seabird species.

The Scomer Island Complex. 415 ha.
West Wales Naturalists' Trust–Royal Society for the Protection of Birds.
This group of islands, including Scomer, Skokholm and Midland Island, form a group at the base of St Bride's Bay.

Grassholm with its famous gannetry is a further 10 kilometres out to sea. Here a spread of Red Fescue covers the hummocked peat much eroded by Puffins – alas now long gone. Today the island is almost solely populated by 22,000 pairs of Gannet, making this the third largest colony in the North Atlantic.

Skokholm, a much larger island, includes the botanical interest of Spring Squill, Danish Scurvy Grass, Thrift, Bluebell, Lesser Celandine and Primrose. Unlike Scomer, neither Common Lizard nor Toad is present. Large numbers of sea-birds breed, including Manx Shearwater, Storm Petrel, Puffin, Guillemot and Razorbill, as well as Ravens.

Scomer is the largest of the islands and perhaps the most accessible. Much of the top surface is heathland where Bluebell, Lesser Celandine, Ground Ivy, Heath Pearlwort, Rock Sea Spurrey and English Stonecrop flourish. Carpets of Thrift, Sea Campion and Sea Squill cover Adder's Tongue, Lanceolate Spleenwort, Wild Madder, Red Goosefoot and Yellow-eyed Grass, but it is the seabirds which are most spectacular. The largest Kittiwake colony in Wales is here, along with a great many Fulmar, Lesser and Greater Black-backed and Herring Gulls, Guillemot and Razorbill. Waders include Curlews, Lapwing and Oystercatcher. Boat trips run daily during the summer when you can visit the island for a few hours. Alternatively, by booking through the West Wales Naturalists' Trust, chalets can be used for a week. Such a visit is well worthwhile because it enables you to be on the islands at night when the vast numbers of Manx Shearwater come into their breeding burrows. During the day however, close views can be had of Puffins at several places on the island and Peregrine, Buzzard and Kestrel join Short-eared Owl as the breeding raptors. Visits to Scomer run from April until September on any day except Monday, when the weather permits.

West Hook Cliffs. SM 762092. 9 ha.
West Wales Naturalists' Trust.
This cliff-top heathland overlooks the

Scomer Island Complex and contains many of the plants found on the islands. It makes an excellent stop-off point for those visitors to the islands as a range of seabirds nest here. The butterflies are also well represented, including Small Pearl-bordered, Dark Green Fritillary, Ringlet and Green Hairstreak.

Glamorgan

Aberthaw Shore. ST 043659. 36 ha. Glamorgan Naturalists' Trust.
This reserve shows a variety of seaside habitats, including a salt marsh and storm beach, but also includes some tall, scrubby, limestone cliffs where Purple Gromwell and Maidenhair Fern can be found. Nesting birds include Raven, and a large population of Adders can be found in the vicinity.

Flatholm. Permit only. 29 ha. South Glamorgan County Council.
This small island in the Bristol Channel is not particularly 'cliffy', and a permit is required for landing (this can be obtained from the Project Manager, Flatholm Project, Harbour Road, Barry). But, in the past large colonies of Lesser Black-backed Gull and Herring Gull dominated the island. Now these have declined, but not to the extent that they allow many other breeding birds. Shelduck, Oystercatcher and some other small species struggle to exist and the island is one of the few places one can find the Wild Leek plant.

Porth Kerry Country Park. ST 092672. 91 ha. Vale of Glamorgan Borough Council.
Maidenhair Fern grows on this limestone cliff which backs onto a shingle beach. Here Sea Beet, Bulbous Foxtail and Yarrow can be found, and the cliff is topped with a wood which has Purple Gromwell, a rare trailing plant with dark purple flowers.

South Gower Coast. Glamorgan Naturalists' Trust, Nature Conservancy Council and National Trust.
This coast encircles the immensely popular Gower peninsula which, although dogged by tourism, is rich in interesting wildlife. The coastal plateau has many bays and coves faced with sand and the surrounding cliffs are both dramatic and beautiful. The rock is predominantly limestone, and the soil supports typical coastal species such as Thrift, Spring Squill, Rock Sea-lavender and Rock and Golden Samphire, together with a host of lime-loving species, such as Common Rock-rose, Carline Thistle and Squinancywort. The area is also one which must have survived glaciation during the last Ice Age, since the isolated Small Restharrow and Goldilocks occur here. Such species seem incapable of spreading and are only found at a few other sites in Britain. Yellow Whitlowgrass grows here and nowhere else in Britain, and other uncommon species include Bloody Cranesbill, Wild Cabbage, Spring Cinquefoil, Hoary Rock-rose and Hutchinsia. Of ornithological interest is Worms Head, a small island which holds the most westerly seabird colonies this side of the Bristol Channel. These include numbers of Guillemot, Razorbill, Fulmar, Kittiwake, Shag and Cormorant. On shore, some of the sea cliffs have caves which contain roosts of the now rare Greater Horseshoe Bat. All in all this area is easily accessible for many people in the south of England and is ideal to explore the rocky shore habitat.

Gwent

This most southerly of the Welsh border counties has foreshore abutting the River Severn. However, none of this is rocky or cliffy in nature and although salt marsh and estuarine habitats can be found here, a short journey across Wales to the ever popular Gower peninsula is needed to find the nearest cliff habitat.

Gwynedd

Bardsey. Permit only. 175 ha.
Bardsey Island Trust.
A permit is required to visit this island and may be booked by telephoning Newton Abbott 68580. Here Spring Squill, gorse, bracken, Sharp Rush, Wilson's Filmy Fern and Lesser Meadow-rue may be found. Rabbits keep the coastal grass short and there is a large population of Manx Shearwaters. Smaller numbers of Kittiwake, Guillemot, Razorbill and Shag occur and Grey Seals can often be seen.

Great Orme Nature Trail. SH 780832. 3–5 km. Aberconwy Borough Council.
These nature trails include an area of limestone grassland with typical limestone flowers, but also top some excellent sea cliffs holding colonies of seabirds. These include Kittiwake, Fulmar, Guillemot, Razorbill, Cormorant, Shag, Chough, Jackdaw and occasionally Raven.

Newborough Warren. SH 406636. 634 ha. Nature Conservancy Council.
Almost all of this reserve is renowned for its extensive sand dunes and associated botanical interest but there is a narrow ridge of rock which runs through Newborough Forest and ends in the tidal island and small rocky outcrops called Ynys Llanddwyn. Some of these tiny islands hold nesting Cormorants and Shags and barely project above the sea surface, whilst the larger island has its acid rocks topped by glacial clays and limey sands, and as such has a good range of plants reflecting this variety of soils.

South Stack Cliffs. SH 205823. 316 ha. Royal Society for the Protection of Birds.
These 120 metre high cliffs hold at least nine breeding species of seabirds, including 2,000 Guillemots, 500 Puffin and 600 Razorbills. These are joined by Carrion Crow, Raven, Jackdaw and Chough, whilst plants characteristic of the western coast include Golden Samphire, Rock Sea Spurrey, Spring Squill and English Stonecrop also occur. Sea Campion forms carpets with Common Scurvy Grass and Grey Seals may also be seen.

Powys

This region has no sea coast but is ideally placed with areas such as Pembrokeshire and the Gower easily accessible for the day-trip investigator.

SCOTLAND

Borders

St Abbs Head. NT 9168. 97 ha. National Trust for Scotland–Scottish Wildlife Trust.
On these lava cliffs 10,000 Guillemots breed, with several thousand Kittiwake and Razorbill, whilst Fulmar nest amongst the Scurvy Grass, Thrift and Sea Campion. Deep recesses in this exhilarating scenery give good views over the colonies and, from some of the headlands, Gannets can be watched flying to and from their Bass Rock breeding ground. Out of the breeding season shearwaters and skuas can also be seen passing these cliffs. Behind the seafront, short grassland rolls down to the Mire Loch in the valley bottom. Here Common Rock-rose, Common Birdsfoot Trefoil, mats of Thyme, Thrift and Spring Sandwort join Tormentil and Milkwort as the botanical interest. Butterflies include Small Copper, Common Blue and Grayling, but other rare migrants have also been found. For many in the north eastern parts of England, with the exception of Bempton Cliffs in Yorkshire and the Farnes in Northumberland, these will be the nearest available spectacular seabird colonies.

Central

Although this region includes no real sea coast, being centrally placed in the Scottish massif, it has the Firth of Forth, and all of the surrounding Scottish rocky shores and cliff-lined coast is within easy reach.

Dumfries and Galloway

Mull of Galloway. NX 157305. 16 ha.
Royal Society for the Protection of Birds.
Spring Squill and Purple Milk Vetch join Roseroot, Scots Lovage, Rock Sea Spurrey, Golden Samphire, Rock Samphire and Rock Sea-lavender on these cliffs which reach a height of 87 metres. They also support a moderate-sized seabird colony, which includes Cormorants, Shags, Kittiwakes, Guillemots, Razorbills and Fulmars.

Fife

Isle of May. NT 6599. 57 ha. Nature Conservancy Council.
To reach this small island in the Firth of Forth take a boat from Crail, Anstruther or Pittenween during the summer when weather permits. There is also limited accommodation on the island (contact Isle of May Booking Secretary, c/o Regent Terrace, Edinburgh, EH7 5BT). A bird observatory has been on the Isle of May since 1934 and the populations of the island's resident seabirds have been constantly monitored since this time. They have shown amazing fluctuations: previously over 8,000 pairs of Terns nested, but by the early 70s these had been replaced by nearly 40,000 Herring and Lesser Blackbacked Gulls. Since then the number of gulls has been reduced and in the late 70s terns again returned to breed on the islands. Puffins too have varied in number: in the 1950s there were only 7 pairs, but now there are nearly 9,000 occupied burrows, stretching to the centre of the island.

Shag too have shown a remarkable increase and currently the number of Fulmars is also increasing. Kittiwake, Guillemot and Razorbill are also present and at the northern tip of the island there is a colony of Grey Seal where normally 300 pups are born each year. Botanically the island shows many typical cliff species.

Grampian

Fowlsheugh. NO 880798. 11 ha. Royal Society for the Protection of Birds.
Here a total of 80,000 pairs of 6 species breed on a single cliff stretching for 1.6 kilometres along the coast. Kittiwake, Guillemot, Razorbill, Fulmar and, at the top of the cliff, Herring Gulls form the bulk of the nesting birds, whilst a few Puffins and Shags eke out an existence in an area not really suitable for them. This is one of the largest seabird colonies on the east of Scotland and deep indentations in the cliff make it easy to observe all parts of the colony without disturbance to the birds or any danger to the observer. As such the site is well worth a visit between May and mid-July.

Long Haven Cliffs. NK 1239. 2.5 km.
Scottish Wildlife Trust.
Nine seabird species breed on these cliffs, in a total of 23,000 pairs of birds, but because of the uneven geology the colony is spread out over the 2.5 kilometres. Herring Gull, Kittiwake and Guillemot nest in scattered groups on the pinky-red granite cliffs and Shag build their nests just clear of the high tide mark. Puffin too nest in small numbers and some areas are carpeted with sheets of Red Campion, cushions of Thrift, Primroses, Violets and Bluebells. Other interesting plant species include Scots Lovage, Burnet Rose and Roseroot.

St Cyrus. NO 7464. 92 ha. Nature Conservancy Council.
This reserve includes a relict cliff which

111

overshadows 4 kilometres of sandy beach. Over 350 flowering plants are recorded here, many at the northern limit of their British distribution. These include night-scented Nottingham Catchfly, Soft Clover, Rough Clover, Great Mullein and Vipers' Bugloss. Joining these are Marjoram, Carline Thistle, Wild Liquorice and Henbane. Also of interest are 13 species of butterfly and over 200 moths. Despite the small area of the reserve up to 47 species of bird have bred including a small colony of Little Terns on the beach and Fulmar and Herring Gull on the cliff. Off shore Grey Seal and Common Porpoise can be seen and Otter tracks have been recorded.

Highland North

Handa. MC 1348. 310 ha. Royal Society for the Protection of Birds.

One of the most famous seabird colonies in the British Isles, the near vertical cliffs, some 140 metres high, which bound Handa on three sides, attract an extraordinary range of birds. Guillemot, Razorbill, Kittiwake, Fulmar, Puffin and Shag share the sheer cliff-faces, whilst 6 lochans in the moorland interior attract a small flock of Barnacle Geese in the winter. Other ornithological interests include Wheatear, and since the mid 1960s colonies of both Great and Arctic Skua. These birds now pester the Shelduck, Eider, Ring Plover and Golden Plover, and their aerobatic displays are of great interest to any visitor. Plants include Deergrass, Heath Spotted and Northern Marsh Orchids, Bog Asphodel, Pale Butterwort, Royal Fern, Few Flowered Spike Rush and Scots Lovage. To gain access to the island a boat runs from Tarbet on the mainland between April and August, weather permitting, and the great stack and its associated seabird colony is a must for any visitors to the north.

Balmacara. MG 7930. 2,274 ha. National Trust for Scotland.

This rugged promontory has rocky coast-line and scattered islands, much of which can be explored by the visitor, if he or she shows the necessary respect for the crofted land which is still in use today. Although no massive seabird colonies exist, scattered numbers of the typical species can be found and the area also holds small populations of the rare and beautiful Dark-red Helleborine.

Lothian

Bass Rock. NT 602873. 10 ha. Privately owned.

This volcanic island rises over 90 metres from the sea and is world famous for its Gannets. Some 9,000 pairs breed on the island and today the colony has outgrown the cliff-sides and has spread onto the sloping summit. Permission to land is obtainable from the local boatman who runs a service from North Berwick during the summer when weather conditions are favourable. Visitors can either circle the island to marvel at the wheeling Gannets, Kittiwakes, Puffins, Guillemots, Razorbills, Shags and Fulmars, or land and explore on foot, at close quarters, all of these birds at their nesting-sites. Such a visit is an ornithological dream *par excellence*. It is especially good for those wishing to photograph the birds since access, if sensibly used, enables you to get very close to the birds.

Forth Islands. Fidra. NO 513867. Eyebroughty. NO 495863. The Lamb. NO 535866. 2 ha. Royal Society for the Protection of Birds.

During summer access to Fidra is by boat, running from North Berwick during good weather; Eyebroughty can be reached by foot at low tide; and The Lamb has no landing access. These island have been relatively recently colonised by Cormorants, Razorbills and Guillemots, and now over 1,000 pairs of Guillemot breed on the reserve. Some 500 pairs of Kittiwake nest on Fidra and the Puffin population has also spread and increased during recent years. Other regularly breeding birds include Shag, Eider, Lesser Black-backed and Herring Gull, along with small numbers of Common and Arctic Tern.

John Muir Country Park. NT 6480. 75 ha. East Lothian District Council.
Although much of this reserve is taken up with an estuary system, and its associated dunes and beach, Whitbury Point and Dunbar Cliffs offer a good vantage point for sea watching, and have a typical range of cliff-top plant species.

Orkney

Copinsay. HY 6001. 152 ha. Royal Society for the Protection of Birds.
This grassy island can be reached by taking a boat from Newark Bay, Lighthouse Pier, or Skaill. During the summer, booking is necessary. (Telephone D. Foubister on Deerness 245, or Deerness 252.) On arrival on the island visitors should proceed first to the information room at the farmhouse. The island has sheer cliffs rising 60 metres high, which hold 30,000 pairs of Guillemot, and 10,000 pairs of Kittiwake, along with several hundred pairs of Fulmar, Razorbill and Great Black-backed Gull. Small numbers of Puffin, Black Guillemot, Shag, Lesser Black-backed, Herring and Common Gull also nest and on Corse of Copinsay, a small offshore island, where a number of Cormorant join Arctic Tern as breeding birds. Botanically, the north coast has particularly abundant Sea Aster and Sea Pearlwort, Sea Spurrey and Sea Spleenwort, which flourish alongside Northern Saltmarsh Grass and Oysterplant.

Marwick Head. HY 2224. 19 ha. Royal Society for the Protection of Birds.
This is the most accessible and easily explored of the seabird colonies in the Orkney Island system. Large numbers of Kittiwake and Guillemot join smaller populations of Razorbill, Fulmar and Puffin on the flat nesting ledges during the summer months. Other birds often encountered include Raven, Jackdaw, Twite and Great and Arctic Skua. Visitors should note that a large part of the colony is invisible from the land and in some places the cliffs are very dangerous. But by correct positioning on the path, which runs to the Kitchener memorial, a good view can be had of the squabbling and noisy seabirds.

Nupe Cliffs, Westray. HY 3950. 14 ha. Royal Society for the Protection of Birds.
This stretch of cliffs runs for 2 kilometres south from Nupe Head, and is possibly the most densely populated seabird colony in Britain. Forty thousand pairs of Guillemot are present and Fulmar, Razorbill and Shag occupy the smaller, detached cliff-ledges. Forty thousand pairs of Kittiwakes also breed on the reserve, with many more non-breeders staking their claim to empty cliff-face sites. Puffins are present in small numbers, and on the heathland behind the cliffs Arctic Skua breed, as do Arctic Terns and several wader species.

Outer Hebrides

Balranald, North Uist. NF 7070. 658 ha. Royal Society for the Protection of Birds.
Only part of this reserve is rocky coastline, since most is covered by a loch and its surrounding marshland. Machair and grassland areas are also found, but the area of cliff is notable for its Shag and Black Guillemot. North Yold has a population of Otters, and these animals can be frequently seen on Balranald's shores and in the loch. The sea of the reserve is also one of the best places in Britain to see porpoises, dolphins and whales.

North Rona and Sula Sgeir. HW 8132 and HW 6230. 138 ha. Nature Conservancy Council.
Permission to land on these islands must

be obtained through Barbas Estates Limited and the Nature Conservancy Council in Inverness must be informed of proposed visits. Both of these remote islands, however, are renowned for their wildlife interest and are worth the trouble. Sula Sgeir rises to 100 metres, and in summer it is white with nesting Gannets. North Rona is a much larger island, where up to 2,000 Grey Seal pups are born each year, and here there are also important colonies of Leach's and Storm Petrel. Both islands also have many breeding Guillemots, Razorbills, Kittiwakes, Puffins and Fulmars.

St Kilda. NA 1000. 846 ha. National Trust for Scotland–NCC.

One of these islands, Hirta, is the remotest inhabited island in British waters and has the highest sea cliff, which towers 430 metres above the sea. The cliffs of the smaller islands reach 360 metres. St Kilda has the largest colony of Fulmars in Britain. Indeed, this group of islands is the most important seabird breeding station in the British Isles. The gannetry on Boreray is the largest in the world with over 50,000 pairs, and although the visitor may appreciate the extraordinary numbers of Guillemot, Puffin, Gannet and Fulmar, those of the Leach's and Storm Petrel and Manx Shearwater will probably go unobserved since these species are active only at night. Several island endemic sub-species occur, such as the St Kilda Wren and the St Kilda Field Mouse. Flocks of the ancient Soay sheep run wild on Soay and Herta, and now considerable numbers of Grey Seal breed on these islands. Cliff vegetation includes Roseroot, Primrose, Honeysuckle, Moss Campion, Purple Saxifrage and rather unexpectedly a species of bryophyte which is more often found in the Mediterranean. This occurs because, although wet and salty, St Kilda's climate is also mild. Now in the hands of the National Trust for Scotland, visiting these islands is much easier than in the past, and several independent charter companies run short trips to the islands, which generally involve sleeping on board the boat.

Shetland

Fair Isle. HZ 2172. 830 ha. National Trust for Scotland.

Now famous for its exceptional numbers of migrational rarities, Fair Isle is most typically covered with that ever-increasing species the common twitcher. Here red sandstone cliffs edge most of the shoreline and rise as high as 200 metres above the sea in places. Large numbers of the typical cliff species are present: Fulmar, Guillemot, Kittiwake and Razorbill join a Gannet colony and some 30,000 pairs of Puffin. At least 100 pairs of Storm Petrel nest here and although Leach's Petrel are occasionally caught on the island they are not yet proven breeders. More than 100 pairs of Arctic Skua and 40 pairs of Great Skua nest here, and most visitors will experience the aggressive displays of these species if they visit the island in the breeding season. Over 200 species of plant are recorded and both Spring Squill and Field Gentian can be found in the white instead of the normal blue forms. Five orchid species occur, including Lesser Twayblade and Frog Orchid, and ferns include Wilson's Filmy Fern, Moonwort and Adder's Tongue.

Fetlar. HU 6091. 699 ha. Royal Society for the Protection of Birds.

Although this island is most famous for the past breeding of Snowy Owls, it also has large populations of many other birds, including many waders, some terns and a concentration of Arctic and Great Skuas. Storm Petrel and Manx Shearwater also nest, but compared to Shetland's other islands the cliff-nesting seabird population is smaller. Puffins are the most numerous seabirds, with around 2,500 pairs on the island, and Black Guillemots and Shags are also widely distributed around the island's shores.

Foula. HT 9639. 1,380 ha.
This island has cliffs rising 370 metres from the sea and its seabird colonies are outstanding. It holds one of the largest and most diverse populations in the North Atlantic and its 3,000 pairs of Great Skua account for half of Shetland's total, and nearly 30 per cent of those breeding in the northern hemisphere. The number of Arctic Skua is small by comparison at 270 pairs and it was on these islands that the first breeding of the Fulmar occurred in 1878. (Now these cliffs hold 40,000 pairs.) Auk totals are also the highest in Shetland with about 35,000 pairs of Puffins, 30,000 pairs of Guillemot, 5,000 Razorbill and 60 pairs of Black Guillemot. Joining these are 3,000 pairs of Shag, 6,000 pairs of Kittiwake and 3,000 pairs of Arctic Tern. Largely unseen, due to their nocturnal behaviour, this massive array of birds is further joined by a 1,000 pairs of Storm Petrel, the largest concentration in Shetland, and is the only proven Shetland breeding site for the rare and elusive Leach's Petrel. In all, 16 species of seabirds nest here with a population of over 125,000 pairs of birds. These numbers are swollen by a great many more non-breeding individuals which join to make this one of the most important seabird stations in the northern hemisphere. Access is by boat from Walls. Details from Lerwick Tourist Office.

Haaf Gruney. HU 6398. 18 ha. Nature Conservancy Council.
Spring Squill and Northern Salt Marsh grass are the botanical interest on this boulder-bleached island, which holds breeding populations of Storm Petrel and Black Guillemot.

Hermaness. HP 6016. 964 ha. Nature Conservancy Council.
The cliffs at this site are the most northerly tip of Britain, and provide several miles of avian activity. Fourteen species of seabird breed here, including important numbers of Skuas, which, with the Gannets, have shown a spectacular increase in recent years. Five thousand pairs of Gannet and over 800 pairs of skua can now be observed from the 200 metre high cliff. Puffins are the most numerous species present with tens of thousands of pairs frequenting the scree slopes. Sixteen thousand pairs of Guillemot, 2,000 pairs of Razorbill and Shag, and a few Black Guillemot join 5,000 pairs of Kittiwake and 10,000 pairs of Fulmar and a single Black-browed Albatross, a lonely lost wanderer from the other end of the globe. The plant life on these acid cliffs is varied, and includes Roseroot and Scots Lovage. A sub-species of Red Campion is present and Otter, Common Seal and Grey Seal can all be seen from this reserve which, like Foula, is one of the most important seabird stations in Europe, if not the world.

Noss. HU 5540. 313 ha. Nature Conservancy Council.
Like Hermaness and Foula this is one of the most spectacular seabird colonies and is of international importance. Huge numbers of Gannet, Guillemot and Kittiwake join over 200 pairs of Great Skua and 40 pairs of Arctic Skua. The cliffs rise nearly 200 metres from the sea and provide countless shelves and nesting-sites for the thousands of wheeling, noisy birds. Plants include Chickweed Wintergreen, Spring Squill, Thrift, Sea and Red Campion, Roseroot and Scurvy Grass. Access to the island in summer is from Lerwick, via the island of Bressay, and is run by the Nature Conservancy Council. During this period a small visitor centre is opened and visitors are asked to stay on the cliff-top path to avoid disturbing the nesting birds.

Yellfound Islands. Permit only. 162 ha. Royal Society for the Protection of Birds.
Steep cliffs at Ramna stacks and Gruney have large seabird populations. Guillemot, Kittiwake and Puffin are joined on the islands by Fulmar, Black Guillemot, Great and Arctic Skuas and Arctic Terns. These islands are also one of the best places to

see Otter in the British Isles, and Common and Grey Seals are regular breeders.

Skye and the Smaller Islands

Eigg. Permit only. 608 ha. Scottish Wildlife Trust Reserve.
At one end of the island the plateau falls away to steep cliffs, some having spectacular pillars, where Buzzard and Raven join Golden Eagle as nesting species. Botanically, Norwegian Sandwort and Roseroot are of interest.

Rhum. NM 3798. 10,684 ha. Nature Conservancy Council.
A permit is required to visit any of the parts of the island away from the loch area, and at the southern edge of the island there are modest seabird colonies which may be worth visiting if you are already on the island.

Strathclyde North

Burg, Mull. NM 426266. 617 ha. National Trust for Scotland.
This site is most famous for the presence of its fossil tree which is embedded in columnar basalt and may only be seen at low tide, yet it is also an area rich in varied plant life.

Caradale. NR 8137. 70 ha. Scottish Wildlife Trust.
This grassy peninsular has low cliffs which give good views over Kilbrannan Sound and from here Otter, Porpoise, Bottle-nosed Dolphin and Killer Whale can be regularly seen in summer, as well as a variety of seabirds.

Strathclyde South

Ailsa Craig. NX 0199. 105 ha.
Ailsa Craig has over 35,000 pairs of nesting seabirds, nearly half of which are Gan-

nets. This colony has been in existence since at least 1526, and was for a long time important as a local source of food. Nearly 2½ kilometres of the west cliffs are occupied by these species where they are joined occasionally by intruding Kittiwake, Guillemot, Razorbill, with smaller numbers of Fulmar, Puffin and Black Guillemot, all trying to pack onto the 150 metre high, vertical cliffs. The mild damp climate also encourages a rich and diverse array of wild flowers, including all of the typical cliff-side species.

Tayside

Seaton Cliffs. NO 667416. 10.5 ha. Scottish Wildlife Trust.
These rich red sandstone cliffs are carpeted with Scurvy Grass, Thrift, Birdsfoot Trefoil, Primroses and Violets and, in the marshier places, by Meadowsweet and Meadow Cranesbill. Marsh Orchid, Early Purple Orchid and Heath Spotted Orchid also occur and the vetches found here include the Purple Milk Vetch. The Scurvy Grass attracts a range of butterflies, including Green-veined White, Common Blue and Meadow Brown, but because the coarse, sandstone cliffs slope seawards they do not provide suitable nest-sites for birds, and consequently there are few seabirds present. During summer, however, Fulmar, Kittiwake and Guillemot can be seen offshore and breeding birds do include Eider.

RIGHT **Limpet tracks**

SOME USEFUL ADDRESSES

Conchological Society of Great Britain and Ireland
51, Wychwood Avenue
Luton LU2 7HT

British Trust for Ornithology
Beech Grove, Tring
Hertfordshire, HP23 5NR

The Mammal Society
Burlington House
Piccadilly
London W1V 0LQ

The Marine Biological Association
The Plymouth Laboratory
Citadel Hill, Plymouth
Devon PL1 2PB

Nature Conservancy Council
Northminster House
Peterborough PE1 1VA

Royal Society for Nature Conservation
The Green, Nettleham
Lincoln LN2 2NR

Royal Society for the Protection of Birds
The Lodge, Sandy
Bedfordshire SG19 2DL

Scottish Marine Biology Association
Dunstaffnage Marine Research
  Laboratory
P.O. Box No. 3, Oban
Argyll PA34 4AD

SAFETY ON THE SHORE

The cliff-side and sea shore is, if not treated with due respect, a dangerous environment for the amateur naturalist to explore. It hopefully goes without saying that at the cliff-top care is needed when close to the edge. Cliffs are constantly being eroded, that is why they are cliffs after all, and even hard rock-ledges are not entirely safe, since the sparse and loose soil is apt to slip off under any pressure. Do not descend to any pseudo-accessible ledges to get a better view of nesting seabirds – get more powerful binoculars or a telescope. Also cliff-top vegetation can be very slippery due to the sea spray. Some species even have naturally waxy leaves, which can be positively 'icy', even on shallow slopes. This brings us to foot-wear; training shoes are not suitable because as soon as their soles are worn they are treacherous when wet and a slip on sea-sprayed grass or seaweed could result in skinned hands and knees or even a 100 metre dive into a rock-pool! Wear stout boots (or wellingtons for rock-pools) which have thick tracked soles. When exploring the shore at the base of cliffs keep your eye on the tide. It can creep in unnoticed when you are absorbed by the antics of an anemone. You could become trapped at the base of the cliffs, which is very dangerous. Proceed between rock-pools carefully; the substrate can be very slippery and some of the lower pools very deep. Lastly, by the time you reach the shore you will not be the first human visitor there, so watch out for broken glass and other dangerous flotsam, and please do not add to it. Take your litter home. Very lastly, do not be a Victorian type of natural-ist and denude the rock-pools of their inhabitants. Most of the animals you find will only live a few hours in anything but a specialised marine aquarium so taking an anemone home in a jam jar is a bit mean.

THE PHOTOGRAPHS

All the photographs in this book were taken using 35 mm SLR Canon cameras (A-1 and F-1) in conjunction with the fol-lowing Canon FD lenses: 28 mm, 50 mm, 70–210 mm zoom, 100 mm macro and 500 mm F8 reflex. They were all taken using Kodachrome 64 slide film using a tri-pod and cable release. In some cases fil-ters have been used (primarily 81B, soft-ener and polarising) to enhance or destroy some aspect of the reality.

BIBLIOGRAPHY

Barrett, J. and **Yonge, C. M.** *The Seashore, A Collins Pocket Guide.* Collins, London, 1958.

Barrett, J. *Life on the Sea Shore.* Collins Countryside Series. Collins, London, 1974.

Bradshaw, M. J. *A New Geology.* Hodder and Stoughton, London, 1968 (reprinted 1977).

Brown, L. *British Birds of Prey.* New Naturalist, Collins, London, 1976.

Burton, R. *Bird Behaviour.* Granada, London, 1985.

Corbet, G. B. and **Southern, H. N.** (Eds) *The Handbook of British Mammals* (2nd Edition), Blackwell Scientific Publications, Oxford, England, 1977.

Cramp, S. and **Simmons, K. E. L.** (Eds) *Handbook of the Birds of Europe, the Middle East and North Africa.* The Birds of the Western Palearctic (7 volumes – 4 published), Oxford University Press, 1977.

Etherington, R. *Plant Physiological Ecology.* Institute of Biology Reader No. 98, Edward Arnold, London, 1978.

Eyre, S. R. *Vegetation and Soils, A World Picture.* Edward Arnold, London, 1968.

Evans, P. G. H. *The Natural History of Whales and Dolphins.* Christopher Helm, London, 1987.

Fuller, R. J. *Bird Habitats in Britain.* T. and A. D. Poyser, Calton, England, 1982.

Harris, M. P. *The Puffin.* T. and A. D. Poyser, Calton, England, 1984.

Harrison, C. *A Field Guide to the Nests, Eggs and Nestlings of British and European Birds.* Collins, London, 1975.

Harrison, R. J. and **King, J. E.** *Marine Mammals* (2nd Edition). Hutchinson, London, 1980.

Heinzel, M., Fitter, R. and **Parslow, J.** *The Birds of Britain and Europe, with North Africa and the Middle East.* Collins, London, 1972.

Hywel-Davies, J. and **Thom, V.** (Eds) *The Macmillan Guide to Britain's Nature Reserves.* Macmillan, London, 1984.

Lack, P. *The Atlas of Wintering Birds in Britain and Ireland.* T. and A. D. Poyser, Calton, England, 1986.

Löfgrens, L. *Ocean Birds. Their Breeding, Biology and Behaviour.* Croom Helm, London and Canberra, 1984.

Major, A. *The Book of Seaweed.* Gordon and Cremonesi, London and New York, 1977.

McClintock, D. and **Fitter, R. S. R.** *A Pocket Guide to Wildflowers.* Collins, London, 1956.

McLeisch, A. *Geology.* Blackie, Glasgow and London, 1978.

Peterson, R., Mountfort, G. and **Hollom, P. A. D.** *A Field Guide to the Birds of Britain and Europe.* Collins, London, 1954 (Enlarged reprint, 1985).

Phillips, R. *Wild Flowers of Britain.* Pan, London, 1977.

Putman, R. J. and **Wratten, S. D.** *Principles of Ecology.* Croom Helm, London, 1984.

Ratcliffe, D. *The Peregrine Falcon.* T. and A. D. Poyser, Calton, England, 1980.

Reade, W. and **Hoskins, E.** *Nesting Birds, Eggs and Fledglings in Colour.* Blandford, London, 1967.

Sharrock, J. T. R. *The Atlas of Breeding Birds in Britain and Ireland.* T. and A. D. Poyser, Calton, England, 1976.

Streeter, D. and **Gerrard, I.** *The Wildflowers of the British Isles.* Macmillan, London, 1983.

Yonge, C. M. *The Seashore.* New Naturalist, Collins, London, 1949.